POLES
IN THE BATTLE
OF BRITAIN

POLES
IN THE BATTLE
OF BRITAIN

A PHOTOGRAPHIC ALBUM OF THE POLISH 'FEW'

PETER SIKORA

AIR WORLD

AIR WORLD

POLES IN THE BATTLE OF BRITAIN
A Photographic Album of the Polish 'Few'

First published in Great Britain in 2020 by
Air World
An imprint of
Pen & Sword Books Ltd
Yorkshire – Philadelphia

ISBN 978 1 52678 241 0

Typeset by SJmagic DESIGN SERVICES, India.
Printed and bound in the UK by TJ International Ltd.

Pen & Sword Books Limited incorporates the imprints of Atlas, Archaeology, Aviation, Discovery, Family History, Fiction, History, Maritime, Military, Military Classics, Politics, Select, Transport, True Crime, Air World, Frontline Publishing, Leo Cooper, Remember When, Seaforth Publishing, The Praetorian Press, Wharncliffe Local History, Wharncliffe Transport, Wharncliffe True Crime and White Owl.

For a complete list of Pen & Sword titles please contact

PEN & SWORD BOOKS LIMITED
47 Church Street, Barnsley, South Yorkshire, S70 2AS, England
E-mail: enquiries@pen-and-sword.co.uk
Website: www.pen-and-sword.co.uk

Or
PEN AND SWORD BOOKS
1950 Lawrence Rd, Havertown, PA 19083, USA
E-mail: Uspen-and-sword@casematepublishers.com
Website: www.penandswordbooks.com

Contents

Introduction

Poland, a country situated in the central – hence fragile part of Europe – has a history stretching back for over 1,000 years. At some point it was known as the Polish Empire and the biggest country in Europe covering 1 million square kilometres from the Baltic Sea to the Black Sea and at different times contained the territories of eighteen countries that exist today, including parts of Czech Republic, Estonia, Finland, Germany, Hungary, Latvia, the whole of Lithuania,[1] Moldova, Rumania, Russia, Slovakia, Sweden or Ukraine and having her colonies in Gambia and Tobago.[2] Yet due to her location Poland was always vulnerable, fighting for her place and for freedom. She also suffered badly in 1939 only to earn her 'First to Fight' sad and unpleasant, rather than glamorous reputation. With less than twenty years of independent existence, and after returning to the European map only in November 1918, Poland was a 'Guinea Pig' type of country, a testing or exercising ground for Hitler and his evil doctrines.[3]

Slavic Poland stood in the way of the Third German Reich, aggressive and hungry for power and with a strategy of ethnical cleanliness that its Wehrmacht had to implement, once the 'Fall Weiss' plan was executed. Fighting a lone war against three official enemies: Nazi Germany, pro-fascist Slovakia and Soviet Russia (not to mention that there were numerous occasions when Ukrainians, who expected Soviets' blessing, have murdered Polish civilians), showing their overwhelming supremacy on land and sea, as well as in the air, Poland and her invasion was an example of how modern

---

1. The Crown of the Polish Kingdom and the Grand Duchy of Lithuania formed the Polish – Lithuanian Commonwealth. Even now, however, some Western historians often call General Tadeusz Kościuszko, who became the Polish national hero, Lithuanian. Polish political leader Marshal Józef Piłsudski was also born in a Polish family settled in Lithuania.
2. Both via Courland that was a vassal state of the Polish-Lithuanian Commonwealth.
3. It is less known that in 1933 Polish leader Marshal Józef Piłsudski proposed to the French a joint preventive war against Germany when Hitler just came to power.

war would be fought. It was an unlearnt lesson for Hitler's future adversaries and targets and clear alert that no country in Europe was safe.

By the outbreak of the Second World War, Poland's Military Aviation, quite commonly and incorrectly called the Polish Air Force by current media,[4] was inferior in every aspect. From having the world's first all-metal built and fastest fighter plane in the mid-1930s, considered for purchase by the RAF as it outperformed British contenders, to flying mostly outdated aircraft in 1939. Polish fliers had no lack of determination though, which was accompanied by bravery and a willingness to fight to the very end.

After the September 1939 catastrophe, those who were able to fight were ordered to evacuate themselves to France in the hope of continuing to fight the enemy in the air. Around 8,000 airmen joined 'Sikorski's tourists' as German propaganda ironically branded the Poles who started their long journey westwards. When France, one of the biggest European players, went down too, quicker than anyone possibly assumed, the Poles realised that there was no place to go other than Great Britain. They called the country of which they had no knowledge at all 'An Island of Last Hope'.

Yet the mistrust was mutual. The British were rather sceptical by then, not believing that the fighting spirit of the Slavic 'invaders' or 'escapees', as they were, and still are, patronisingly called, undermined by two lost campaigns, would keep them going for so long. Underestimating their skills and potential, initially the Royal Air Force allowed only two light bomber squadrons consisting of Polish personnel (including fighter pilots!) to be formed. Poles had to learn English first, study King's Regulations and eventually get a grip on how to fly aircraft very much different from any others they had flown in Poland and France. In short, they had to adapt to opposite drill – completely different to what was known to continental airmen. Operating a throttle located on the other side of the cockpit, and working in the opposite direction to any continental instrument they knew, was only the tip of the iceberg. Converting from metres and kilometres to feet, yards and miles also caused a headache.[5] Their English was improving slowly yet they managed to charm the local girls by using the very first and

---

4. In pre-war Poland its Military Aviation known as *Lotnictwo* or *Lotnictwo Wojskowe*, was an integral part of the Armed Forces and reported directly to Army orders (unlike Royal Air Force). The first attempt to call it *Polskie Siły Powietrzne* (PAF) was made in France and then officially used in Britain.

5. Although miles, known as 'Polish miles' (1 m = 7,146 metres in the eighteenth century, and 1m = 8,534 metres since 1819), were used in old times too.

INTRODUCTION

'crucial' words they learnt: 'Me Polish, I love you.' (With the word 'Polish' being pronounced exactly as in 'shoe polish', hence initially difficult to understand.)

There was also a struggle at higher level. What to do with these Poles? There was no law to allow foreigners to form their own military forces on British soil. It was initially decided to place Polish airmen in the Volunteer Reserve of the RAF. However, on 5 August 1940, Winston Churchill and General Władysław Sikorski agreed that the Polish Air Force would be an integral part of the Polish Armed Forces in Exile. This decision was followed by the British Parliament's legislation (known as an Allied Forces Act) that constituted legal status of the PAF as an independent military aviation of Poland operating under operational command of the RAF. Soon after all the Polish airmen left the VR and joined the ranks of their very own Polish Air Force. Meanwhile, many of the impatient Poles had already started training in the air while some of them, upon completion, were posted to RAF Squadrons. Time for mistrust was almost over, Great Britain needed men capable of flying Spitfires, Hurricanes or Wellingtons.

Two Polish bomber squadrons, Nos. 300 and 301 were formed on 1 and 22 July 1940 respectively, while two fighter squadrons started getting in shape too. These were 302 'City of Poznań' at RAF Leconfield and 303 'Tadeusz Kościuszko City of Warsaw' at RAF Northolt. The first one was created on 13 July, while the second one took shape on 2 August. There were two other Polish bomber squadrons formed in August 1940. These were No. 304 on 22 August and No. 305 a week later, but neither saw action during the Battle of Britain. Additional Polish fighter squadrons were also organised, including No. 306 on 28 August, No. 307 on 24 August, No. 308 on 9 September, but again, none of these were engaged in combat flying during the summer and early autumn of 1940. The last Polish unit formed in 1940, initially as No. 309 Army Co-operation Squadron, was organised on 10 October.

A group of 145 Polish fighter pilots who were officially considered to have fought during the Battle of Britain, the largest non-British contingent, consisted of a mixture of airmen with various backgrounds, careers and combat experiences. On one side there were fliers such as Pilot Officer Stanisław 'Curly' Skalski (still relatively young but with four kills already confirmed over Poland) or Flight Lieutenant Franciszek 'Agnes' Jastrzębski (with three kills). On another side there were men like Flying Officer Tadeusz 'Bald-headed' Nowierski (ex-light bomber pilot who fought over Poland), or Pilot Officer Stefan Stegman with no combat experience whatsoever.

There was also a distinctive age difference between them from Squadron Leader Mieczysław 'King of the Castle' Mümler, born in the nineteenth century, to Sergeant Michał Brzezowski who was killed just two months before his twentieth birthday. There were former *Eskadra* (equivalent of Squadron) or *Dywizjon* (equivalent of Wing) commanders among the Polish Few, such as Flying Officers Wieńczysław Barański, Juliusz Frey or Squadron Leader Zdzisław 'King' Krasnodębski, as well as former flying instructors such as Flying Officer Jan Czerny, Flying Officer Witold 'Cobra' Urbanowicz or experienced but not battle-hardened experimental and test pilots, including Flying Officers Wilhelm Pankratz, Antoni Ostowicz and Pilot Officer Zbigniew Oleński.

Despite two Polish fighter squadrons being under intensive training and eventually posted for operational duties, a quite significant number of Poles also reinforced over twenty RAF Squadrons. This caused a lot of disadvantages, from flying alone or in small groups among English speaking colleagues, to struggling with the British aerial tactics, which Poles considered to be obsolete. Also the Poles could not support each other morale-wise, which was a crucial factor at the time. Fighting side by side with old friends, feeling safer and being protected by the men they knew, properly understood and they trusted, while shooting the enemy, was what they preferred. Despite these disadvantages they were quickly adopted (often as a squadron's mascot – in a non-patronising way of course!), accepted and admired. There were over seventy Polish pilots flying in RAF squadrons and they shot down nearly eighty enemy aircraft.

Most of the operational Polish pilots flew Hurricanes during the Battle of Britain serving in the following Squadrons: 3, 17, 32, 43, 56, 79, 85, 111, 145, 151, 213, 229, 238, 249, 253, 257, 302, 303, 501, 601, 605, 607 and 615. A relatively smaller group was posted to Spitfire Squadrons: 54, 65, 74, 152, 234, 603 and 609. Only one man, Sergeant Jan Rogowski (Nos. 74 and 303), flew both types operationally during the Battle of Britain.

Although the language barrier caused a lot of issues at the beginning, the Poles of 302 and 303 found a solution by using their own language in the air. Despite British frustration and reprimands, this was the easiest way to communicate when on a mission and therefore the simplest method of keeping their comrades aware of possible danger. Instead of thinking 'what does this bloody command mean in English', they simply shouted *'Niemcy z dołu'* or *'Niemcy za tobą'* ('Germans below' or 'Germans behind you') and their action was immediate!

INTRODUCTION

The Poles saw many horrible scenes of brutality and inhumanity back in Poland, civilians being targeted and killed, towns and villages pounded with bombs and destroyed. They left their loved ones behind, often wives, children, certainly mothers, sisters or brothers to fight over a thousand miles away, unsure of their safety and lives. This only fuelled their hatred of the enemy, their determination. These deep-seated feelings helped them tremendously by making the task of eliminating every target with black crosses that was in their reach, more desired. These feelings provided the incentive to get in as close as possible to make sure that their opponent couldn't return for refuelling, or in the best case – wouldn't be able to breathe anymore.

At the same time 'The other Battle of Britain', perhaps better known as 'The Battle of the Barges' was being fought across the Channel. Although there is still an argument among historians, whether 'Bomber Boys' played any part in the Battle of Britain and therefore should qualify as 'The Few', it seems to be obvious that their actions prevented the German invasion fleet from relaxing while waiting calmly for the result of air encounters to execute operation 'Sea Lion'. Both Polish bomber squadrons – 300 and 301 – were employed in that part of defence during September and October 1940, by providing 62 operational airmen each and increasing the total number of Poles engaged in operations to 269.

It is officially claimed that 145 Polish fighter pilots flew operationally during the Battle of Britain – the author believes this to be 146. Of those 'Polish Few', thirty were killed during this period. Despite the 'over claiming' controversy which concerns both sides of the conflict, the official score reported by seventy-nine of the Polish pilots who made claims during that time is recorded as 203 1/2 enemy aircraft destroyed, a further thirty-five destroyed probably and thirty-six damaged. Apart from these statistics, the Polish effort and engagement varied from 113 operational sorties flown by Flying Officer Stefan Witorzeńć to just one mission performed by twenty-two of the Poles. Gradually they participated in all phases of the Battle of Britain, achieving their first success on 19 July. It is crucial to note that in the most difficult period of the Battle of Britain, Poles accounted for 13 per cent of the total number of Fighter Command pilots involved in fighting, and by October 1940 this had risen considerably to 20 per cent! Not bad for the foreign 'Few'!

It would be unjust to say that No. 303 Squadron's success came without the influence of two British and one Canadian pilot. They combined to claim sixteen enemy aircraft destroyed, ten probably destroyed and one damaged out of the squadron's total 126 kills. Sergeant Josef František should be mentioned too, as he is a more complicated case. Despite being a Czechoslovak citizen, in 1939 he consciously chose to be part of the Polish Military Aviation and is still considered 'one of us' by the Poles. Erroneously called 'a guest of 303 Squadron', this flying maverick gained seventeen kills before he was killed in a landing accident.

By comparison, No. 302 'City of Poznań' Squadron's achievements were less spectacular and directly linked to two crucial factors. Its location in 12 Group meant this Polish unit operated further from the main region of fighting, and being part of Duxford Wing, 302 were often prevented from reaching the combat area in time. Both played a vital part in their performance. Nonetheless, there is no doubt that the quality, skills and experience of pilots of both units were equally the same.

The Polish airmen who flew over Britain and the English Channel during the summer and autumn of 1940 spoke a language almost unheard of before. They hated British medium-rare lamb, perhaps they even looked differently. However they came to 'The Island of Last Hope' to fight for 'your freedom and ours', as their forefathers had done many times in the past. It is in the Polish blood to support others who are facing the darkest hours of their history in their fight for a freedom more important than life or death.

Acknowledgements

Photos and documents reproduced in this book, as well as essential help, were kindly provided by: Dr Bartłomiej Belcarz, Battle of Britain Memorial Trust, the Borowski family, Nina Britton-Boyle, Melvin Brownless, Andrzej Brzezina, the late Stanisław Chałupa, Zbigniew Charytoniuk, Mark Crame, the late Michał Cwynar, Peter Devitt, Peter and Tony Drobiński, Zenon Dudek, the late John 'Tim' Elkington, Arkady Fiedler Museum & Marek Fiedler, Brendan Finucane QC, Anton and Stefan Gabszewicz, the late Antoni Głowacki, the late Czesław Główczyński, Zenon Gmur, Chris Goss, Stefan Gnyś, Steve Gorzula, Franciszek Grabowski, Łukasz Gredys, Robert Gretzyngier, Julian Evan-Hart, Mark Hillier, the Kellett family, Alexandra Kent, Glenn Knoblock, Dr Tomasz Kopański, the late Franciszek Kornicki, Julian Roch Kowalski Jr., the late Mieczysław Kowalski, Anna Kozłowska-Ryś for the Bajan family, the late Tadeusz Kumiega, Jan Łaguna, the Łapka family, Janina Dunmil-Malinowska, Gina Love Markiewicz, Wojtek Matusiak, Teresa Mümler-Pond, National Digital Archives, the Neyder family, Sofia Niemiec, Dorota Nowakowska for the Łapkowski family, Polish Aviation Museum Cracow, Richard Popek, Roman Popławski, Paul Raymond Ostaszewski, Aleksander Rutkiewicz, Andy Saunders, the late Stanisław Skalski, the late Stanisław Socha, Dr Grzegorz Śliżewski, the late Czesław Tarkowski, Andrew Thomas, the Topolnicki family, Paweł Tuliński, Witold Urbanowicz jr., the late Floyd Williston, the Wodecki family, Jan Wojciechowski, the Wójtowicz family, the Wren family, the Wydrowski family, Kelvin Youngs, the late Janusz Żurakowski.

This book could not have been completed without the valuable assistance of my good and long-time friend Rodney Byles. As always I would like to thank my wife Maggie for her patience. On this occasion she influenced this book in a special way, as it was her idea to name it 'Poles in the Battle of Britain'. Love you!

Chapter 1

Into the Dark

Lieutenant Antoni Ostowicz (far left) was a fighter pilot who, alongside Lieutenant Władysław Nowak (in the middle) and Corporal Jan Kremski (right), represented the 2nd Air Regiment and won the prestigious first place during the Central Fighter Competition in Toruń. The picture was taken on 10 October 1937 when the trio of III/2 Fighter Dywizjon (which was similar to an RAF Wing) received the main prize. When the war broke out, Ostowicz was flying with a Prototype Flight and with no chance for combat. Instead he was given a task of evacuating aircraft of the Independent Experimental Air Squadron. He is best known by historians mostly as the first Pole who reported an aerial victory during the Battle of Britain. Sadly, he was also the first Polish pilot killed in action over England.

PZL P.11a as well as its twin 'c' version was the Polish 'first-line' fighter plane of the 1939 Campaign. Here is an aircraft No. 4 with the serial number 7.14 from 113th Fighter Squadron (IV/1 Fighter Wing / 1st Air Regiment in Warsaw) that was photographed on 30 April 1939. This unit was commanded by Lieutenant Wieńczysław Barański, who fought over Britain from 1940.

INTO THE DARK

Opposite above: An interesting photo of 2nd Air Regiment fighter and aerobatic team of pilots upon their return from Rumania in 1933 with Captain Jerzy Bajan (winner of the 1934 Challenge contest) in the middle and PZL P.7 aircraft as the backdrop. Most of them in 1940 participated in the Battle of Britain, including Lieutenant Antoni Wczelik (1st), Lieutenant Jan Czerny (2nd), Lieutenant Bronisław Kosiński (5th) and Corporal Karol Pniak (7th). Captain Kazimierz Niedźwiecki (3rd) was in charge of the group of pilots who in 1939 went to Rumania expecting delivery of aircraft from France and Great Britain. He was also initially planned to be the first Polish commander of No. 302 Squadron in Britain. Sadly Niedźwiecki was unable to complete this task as he was killed in a flying accident prior to this post, while in 6 OTU. His Hurricane I 324 (L1887) collided with Hurricane L2082 piloted by Sergeant Dudley McGee, who was also killed.

Below: Corporal Antoni Markiewicz went into the Battle of Britain with significant combat experience gained initially in Poland, where he flew with 122nd Fighter Squadron and then in France, where he joined 1/145 'City of Warsaw' Squadron. In total he claimed three shared victories over Poland and a further two shared in France. Here he is sitting in the middle, with blond hair, while playing cards with other airmen, and looking straight into the camera. This is quite an unusual view, according to his daughter, as he was very shy of cameras. This can be confirmed by the short film recorded during the Battle of Britain that shows the whole of 302 Squadron singing. Markiewicz, who again is sitting in this footage, is avoiding any eye contact with the recording camera. Note distinctive white 'paper horse' emblem, which was 122nd Fighter Squadron's badge, as well as individual number 6, both visible on PZL P.11's fuselage.

3

Creativity of Polish airmen can be seen in this picture of Sub Lieutenant Jan Dzwonek photographed right before the outbreak of war. He designed this colourful personal emblem of a turkey that was applied on PZL P.11c aircraft from 161st Fighter Squadron of 6th Air Regiment in Lwów. He also flew this aircraft No. 4 in combat even though the rest of his squadron's aircraft were carrying 161's official emblem of white ermine with red wings. Despite being wounded in combat earlier on 2 September, Dzwonek continued flying that day until he met his final fate when he clashed with a formation of Bf 110s. Badly burned, with serious wounds to his head, hand and leg, he bailed out and was hospitalised. This prevented him from leaving Poland, hence after convalescence he joined the Polish Home Army. It is believed that he was a victim of Leutnant Helmut Lent from I./ZG76, who less than a year later flew during the Battle of Britain before being posted for night fighter duties. On 15 August 1940 Lent and his comrades engaged a formation of Fighter Command pilots including Pilot Officer Janusz Żurakowski (as Dzwonek, he was also an ex-161st Fighter Squadron pilot) and Flying Officer Piotr Ostaszewski-Ostoja, from 234 and 609 Squadrons respectively. These two Poles were each credited with the destruction of a Bf 110.

PZL P.11 fighter planes of the 1st Air Regiment in Warsaw, photographed in 1939 during display at Warsaw Okęcie airfield, which was this Regiment's peacetime base. The majority of them are carrying the 'Kościuszko' badge of 111th Fighter Squadron including nos. 3, 10 and 5. Aircraft no. 1 from twin 112th Fighter Squadron with a 'Fighting Cockerel' emblem (in England this badge was adopted by No. 315 Polish Squadron) is also visible. PZL P.37 'Łoś' (Elk) Polish built bomber can be seen in the foreground. PZL P.11c no. 3 was flown by Sub Lt Jerzy Palusiński on 1 September, 1939 when he claimed the first victory for 111th Fighter Squadron also becoming its first loss. After recovering from his wounds he managed to travel to England where he joined 303 Squadron and participated in the Battle of Britain. Note how differently Polish Military Aviation symbols are applied on aircrafts' tails and on the hangars' walls.

INTO THE DARK

Above: This picture of a PZL P.11 covered in hay was taken on 10 September 1939 at Młynów airfield. The quite common myth that all Polish aircraft were destroyed on the ground within the first hours or days of the Polish Campaign can definitely be overruled. Although many non-operational planes were hit during the first raids, in anticipation of war the majority of fighter aircraft, as well as any other first-line machines, were moved from their usual bases and spread all over the country and operated from well-hidden advanced landing grounds...

Opposite above: Typical unsymmetrical application of the Polish Military Aviation symbols of red and white chequer is clearly visible in this photograph. The quite distinctive and characteristic face of Corporal Karol Pniak, a pre-war fighter and aerobatic pilot can be recognised. Pniak claimed two kills followed by two shared victories and more than one enemy aircraft damaged during the Polish Campaign. After arriving in Britain he complained about British combat techniques, yet managed to shoot down three German planes, probably two others, and damaged 1½. All this while flying with No. 32 Squadron RAF in the summer of 1940.

Opposite below: Sub Lieutenant Władysław Gnyś is best known as the first Allied pilot who achieved aerial success during the Second World War. Although his first kill (or rather kills) are clouded in mystery, it is officially believed that it was he who shot down Dornier Do 17E from 7./KG77, which then collided with its wingman, and both crashed at Żurada village near Olkusz. Both crews of Unteroffizier Oskar Finke's aircraft: Unteroffizier Kurt Klose, Gefreiter Wilhelm Annsen and Oberfelwebel Hans Pitch's aircraft: Unteroffizier Georg Reindl, Unteroffizier Josef Ruess were killed. Gnyś fought in the Battle of Britain after joining 302 'City of Poznań' Squadron. Note 3Z+FR code letters of the Finke's aircraft wreckage photographed in Żurada.

Above: ...being lost very soon in combat as this PZL P.11c No. 3 flown by Lieutenant Tadeusz Jeziorowski, a Tactics Officer of III/6 Fighter Wing in Lwów. On 4 September 1939 this aircraft was shot down by German fighters while taking off from Łódź-Widzew and its pilot was killed.

Opposite above: A lesser-known chapter of history. During the invasion of Poland in 1939, the Luftwaffe was supported by the pro-fascist Slovak Air Force (*Slovenské Vzdušné Zbrane*). Note the Letov Š-328 reconnaissance aircraft adorned with German crosses as well as Slovakian symbols, both used during that period. A Dornier Do 17 can be seen in the background. Nevertheless not all Slovaks approved of German rules. During the Battle of Britain Krupina born Sergeant Jozef Káňa flew with No. 303 Polish Squadron.

Opposite below: A battle worn PZL P.11c No. 10 8.70 with notable 'Flying Owl' unit badge (in Britain adopted by No. 316 Polish Squadron) usually flown by Sub Lieutenant Hieronim Dudwał of 113th Fighter Squadron, Pursuit Brigade. This aircraft is being inspected by German troops after capturing an advanced landing ground at Poniatów. Please note (L–R) machine gun attachment, radio and first aid compartment covers all open. Damaged propeller and power plant are visible as well as the dorsal fairing (previously with the luggage access) behind the headrest that was damaged in combat on 1 September, and was ad hoc repaired by the ground crew using unpainted aluminium. The pilot of this aircraft was evacuated to France where he was killed in combat on 7 June 1940, with four confirmed kills to his account. Dudwał was most probably shot down by Feldwebel Rudolf Täschner of JG2, who later fought in the Battle of Britain.

9

Above: Flying personnel of the 4th Air Regiment from Toruń, photographed in Salon, after evacuation to France in 1939. Five of these pilots participated in the Battle of Britain. Standing from left are: Karol Pniak (1st), Franciszek Czajkowski (3rd), Władysław Różycki (5th); sitting: Paweł Zenker (1st) and Stanisław Skalski (3rd). Tadeusz Rolski (seated 2nd) previously commanded III/4 Fighter Wing during the Polish Campaign, in Britain he was appointed first commander of 306 'City of Toruń' Squadron formed during the Battle of Britain.

Opposite above: German troops at the airfield of the Aviation Technical Institute in Warsaw during examination of a captured prototype of a PWS-33 'Wyżeł' (Pointer Dog) of which mass production was already scheduled by the Poles. This rather small aircraft was designed for training the bomber crews. A 7.9 mm front machine gun is visible as well as both PZInż. Major 4B engines. There were pilots employed by the Aviation Technical Institute, such as Captain Wilhelm Pankratz or Lieutenant Zbigniew Oleński, who fought in the Battle of Britain.

Opposite below: The final blow that sealed Poland's fate. On 17 September 1939 Soviet forces invaded from the East. This photograph shows Red Army troops at Wilno-Porubanek airfield of the Wilno Aero club with captured PWS-26 trainers. One of them is carrying number '4', while the aircraft in the background has the serial number 81.261. Both are painted in silver. The Soviets were only able to capture unserviceable aircraft with the others being evacuated to Latvia. Porubanek was to be the base for the planned 7th Air Regiment.

Above: This picture, taken on 27 March 1940 at Lyon-Bron airfield, France at 11.00 when General Władysław Sikorski, Commander in Chief of the Polish Armed Forces, inspected Polish Fighter Sections of the so-called 'Montpellier Group' before they flew for attachment to French squadrons. Quite a significant group of sixty Polish pilots, who later participated in the Battle of Britain, flew operationally in France. They included Sub Lieutenant Wacław Król (in the middle) and Corporal Eugeniusz Nowakiewicz (far right), both standing in the small Section No. 6 on the left. They are wearing Polish peaked caps with winged air force eagle and ranks and both looking at the General and saluting. These pilots, commanded by Lieutenant Władysław Goettel, were posted to GCII/7. Sikorski was accompanied by (L–R) General Józef Zając, commander of the Polish Military Aviation, General Victor Denain, Colonel Stefan Pawlikowski (after arriving in Britain he was appointed Polish Liaison Officer with Fighter Command; he is wearing Polish long flying jacket) and General Louis Picard. Morane Saulnier MS 406 aircraft with the Polish marks rotated 90° are in the background.

Opposite above: The Polish Aviation Training Centre was formed at Lyon – Bron followed by Training Fighter Flight, which was organised on 21 May 1940 to defend the school. Some of the future Battle of Britain pilots were posted to this unit, including Wieńczysław Barański, Jan Borowski, Aleksander Gabszewicz, Bogusław Mierzwa, Włodzimierz Miksa, Jerzy Radomski and Tadeusz Sawicz. Gabszewicz was credited with the destruction of an He 111, while Barański and Radomski downed another aircraft of the same type. Note the Morane Saulnier MS 406 C1 No. 3, photographed at Bron with Bloch MB 131 bomber flying above. Aircraft of the latter type were also flown by the Poles in France. Please note that the version of the Polish Military Aviation chequer applied here is not in accordance with the pre-war regulations (1 December 1918 and 1 March 1930) which stated that the top left and bottom right squares should be in red, despite the fact that even before the war the application was treated individually by some units. This 90°, or in other words 'mirror inconsistency', can often be seen throughout the rest of the war.

A group of Polish pilots with their commander Major Zdzisław Krasnodębski (4th from right) which, as many other groups flying alongside French airmen, was posted to defend France; in this case to GCI/55. First from the left is Sub Lieutenant Jan Zumbach with Corporals Marian Bełc and Stanisław Karubin standing 1st and 2nd from right respectively. Over two months later all of them joined 303 Squadron and fought during the Battle of Britain.

Sub Lieutenant Władysław Gnyś of GCIII/1 (standing 2nd from left), another soon-to-be Battle of Britain pilot who is best known for the first Allied victory of the Second World War. Lieutenant Kazimierz Bursztyn (Polish Section commander) is 3rd from right and his Morane MS 406 C1 No. 1031 L-621 'I' is in the background. Bursztyn made a crash landing in Holland on 12 May 1940 in this aircraft after being shot up in the engine by a He 111. With a knee wound he returned to Belgium only to be killed in action two weeks later.

Chapter 2

The Last Rampart

Some of the Poles felt impatient in France and therefore chose the English way of dealing with war. Those who arrived in Britain prior to the French catastrophe got their uniforms sorted, including RAF greatcoats and service dress hats. However, as the influx of the Polish airmen to Britain continued to increase, some of them pictured here are still lacking their RAF kits. After closer inspection of this photo taken on 25 February 1940 at RAF Eastchurch, which was appointed the very first Polish Air Force Centre, we can see that some of the new arrivals in the second line are still wearing civilian clothes combined with Polish long leather flying jackets. Despite British tailors (including Gieves Ltd) busy making uniforms, the issue was still far from being resolved, hence more discrepancies will be seen in further photos. Sadly, some of these men in this photograph were lost, hence 'ś.P' (RIP) marks can be seen here and there.

Secretary of State for Air, Sir Howard Kingsley Wood welcomes Polish airmen arriving from France. Note that all of them, including Stanisław Skalski, who is standing 2nd from right, are wearing Polish long leather flying coats.

Opposite below: Although at this early stage, all the Polish flying personnel members were only expected to wear the King's Crown RAF padded wings (pilots) or half brevets (observers and air gunners), here General Władysław Kalkus, Deputy Commander of the PAF, is clearly seen as an exception. He is proudly wearing his Polish wings 'gapa' pinned to a 1936 grey Polish uniform made in France.

Below: The initial arrival of Polish airmen caused complications for the British government. The formation, or in this case the reformation, of a foreign air force was a first on British soil and relevant legislation was urgently needed. Meanwhile it was decided that all Polish airmen arriving in Britain between the winter of 1939 and spring of 1940 had to join the Voluntary Reserve of the Royal Air Force. Hence the brass 'VR' badges on Flight Lieutenant Stanisław Brzezina's collar. It was also decided that all Polish officers, regardless of their previous ranks, would need to start from the Pilot Officer level. Interestingly, both Poles in this photo do not fit into this requirement. Brzezina was appointed Polish Commander of the small Polish Air Force Centre at RAF Manston (satellite base to RAF Eastchurch which was already overcrowded with Poles), hereafter his rank instantly rose to Acting Flight Lieutenant. Carrying gas masks was mandatory, and all of the airmen are shown with their respirator haversacks.

Above: Wing Commander Roman Rudkowski during his inspection of Polish airmen at Eastchurch. On the right side are Flight Lieutenant Stanisław Brzezina, Pilot Officer Tadeusz Kawalecki, Pilot Officer Ludwik Martel and Flying Officer Witold Urbanowicz standing in front of their men. Kawalecki and Martel seem to be short of the PAF eagle on their left breast pocket. Interestingly, some of the Polish lower-rank men on the left are wearing RAF 1919 uniforms. It was supposed to be a temporary solution caused by the lack of more adequate equipment, yet this type of uniform can be still seen in photos taken in late September. Brzezina, Kawalecki, Martel and Urbanowicz fought during the Battle of Britain, while Rudkowski commanded Polish 301 (bomber) Squadron during the so called 'Battle of the Barges'.

Opposite above: The initial intention was to form two Polish light bomber squadrons and transfer 2,300 Polish personnel from France. These included equally bomber crews, fighter pilots and ground crews. Fighter pilots, such as Stanisław Skalski and Karol Pniak (4th and 5th from left respectively) were frustrated by the French apathy and indifference to fight, hence they came to Britain even if that would mean flying Fairey Battles, known as 'flying coffins'.

Opposite below: In May 1940 it was obvious that the danger of German raids against RAF Eastchurch was inevitable, therefore all the PAF personnel were withdrawn and transferred to Blackpool. This town became the permanent Polish Air Force Depot, also known as PAF Centre. From left to right are: Pilot Officer Mieczysław Gorzula, Flight Lieutenant Stanisław Brzezina, Flight Lieutenant Stefan Knappe (Medical Officer) and Flying Officer Michał Stęborowski, they all seem to be enjoying the British spring, after leaving the railway station and before being loaded into Thomas Tilling buses. PAF winged eagle badges are clearly visible. Despite being silver colour back in Poland, here, in Britain, it was decided to match the RAF buttons, therefore the silver eagle was surrounded by the golden hussars' wings.

Polish airmen, full of energy and high hopes, lined up on the promenade in Blackpool, spring 1940.

At first, Polish airmen used their energy to seduce girls in Blackpool. Here, Pilot Officer Mieczysław Gorzula makes the first attempts to local beauty…

…which shortly makes him a tourist attraction!

he also has his followers, such as Pilot Officer Jerzy Solak.

After the collapse of France the majority of the Polish airmen were evacuated to England. In this picture taken upon arrival, are personnel from the former Polish 'City of Warsaw' Squadron, also known as GC 1/145. Some of these airmen, who are wearing either grey or dark blue 1936 Polish pattern uniforms made in France, with Polish pilots' badges as well as French Air Force badges and Polish ranks, ended up in operational units during the Battle of Britain, often being posted without conversion to Hurricanes or Spitfires. Time was running out! From left to right are: Julian Kowalski (1), Tadeusz Czerwiński (2), Piotr Łaguna (3) – all three joined 302 Squadron, Juliusz Frey (6) was posted to 607 Squadron while Witold Żyborski (7) and Zygmunt Wodecki (11) went to 303 Squadron as its Adjutant and Medical Officer respectively. Zbigniew Wróblewski (12) and Czesław Główczyński (14) were also posted to 302 Squadron.

Another interesting photo showing Polish airmen upon their arrival in Britain during the summer of 1940. All of them are wearing uniforms of Polish pattern made in France in both colours: Polish grey and French dark blue. Lieutenant Ludwik Paszkiewicz is standing 3rd from left in 2nd row, while Sub Lieutenant Jan Zumbach is 1st from right in 3rd row. The latter is also wearing a PAF Cadet Officers' School badge pinned to his left breast pocket, as well as a French Air Force badge. Both joined 303 Squadron at Northolt soon after this photo was taken. Most of these men have their characteristic Polish pilot's badges, known also as 'gapa', of a flying eagle holding a laurel wreath in its beak (only 1st Class badges looked like this). These badges were made of silver or metal, with the wreath painted in green once the pilot had his baptism of fire. Some of the Polish fliers, despite border checks, managed to smuggle their precious badges from Poland to France; these were made by Warsaw based Jan Knedler. In France these badges were manufactured by Arthus Bertrand & Cie and Aguis Lyon. Upon arrival in the UK the real mass production started and was carried out by various craftsmen until the PAF was disbanded. They were Filski London, J.R. Gaunt & Son, Spink & Son Ltd London and Firmin London. Despite this, some of the Poles stuck with their original badges.

Above: The German invasion was expected in the summer of 1940 and the Poles were getting ready. Some of them came to England with innovative 'defensive' equipment, others found clubs like this one in British storerooms.

Opposite above: Despite initial British reluctance, Deputy Chief of the Air Staff AVM Sholto Douglas insisted on using Polish fighter pilots gathered in Blackpool. On 1 June 1940 the British Air Ministry contacted the Poles, asking whether they were prepared to post 20 or 30 of their pilots to OTUs and then to RAF fighter squadrons. By then the Poles in Britain had only twenty-five fighter pilots with combat experience plus a further forty-five fighter pilots with operational experience available, followed by fifty battle-hardened bomber pilots and ninety bomber pilots who previously flown operationally. Pilot Officer Janusz Żurakowski (right) flew in combat already, defending the Air Force Training Centre in Dęblin, and hopelessly chasing German bombers. Soon after this picture was taken, he proved himself in the Battle of Britain.

English, King's Regulations … everything was back to front here. Please note the Polish makeshift signs: 'Nie palić' (No smoking) or 'Nie śmiecić' (No littering). Eventually Pilot Officer Skalski (1st from right) was posted to the newly formed 302 'City of Poznań' Squadron that was undergoing its first steps, yet he proved to be difficult to manage as he complained about not being sent to a combat unit.

Pilot Officer Stanisław Łapka (standing 2nd from right) was posted to 15 EFTS in Redhill together with Polish bomber crewmen, prior to reporting to 18 OTU in Hucknall. Eventually his fighter fate was 'saved' after he was posted to 6 OTU in Sutton Bridge and then to 302 Squadron. Once the 'Dynamo' operation was concluded the 15 EFTS was transferred to Carlisle.

Above and opposite above: A group of Polish pilots during their stay in 6 Operational Training Unit in Sutton Bridge: (L–R) Flying Officer Witold Urbanowicz (3), Pilot Officer Stanisław Skalski (5) and Flying Officer Stefan Witorzeńć (6).

The last days before posting for combat. Two AF Cadet Officers' School 9th entry classmates: Pilot Officer Paweł Niemiec and Pilot Officer Kazimierz Łukaszewicz accompanied by Pilot Officer Skalski. Łukaszewicz (in the middle) was posted to 501 Squadron RAF where he was killed in action on his second sortie on 12 August 1940. Niemiec (1st from left) flew with 17 Squadron RAF throughout the Battle of Britain claiming the damage to two Do 17s.

Awaiting their postings are (L–R): Flying Officer Witold Urbanowicz (soon to join 145 Squadron RAF), Flying Officer Stefan Witorzeńć (501 Squadron RAF) and Flying Officer Piotr Ostaszewski-Ostoja (609 Squadron RAF).

Another group of Poles. (L–R) are: Pilot Officers Józef Kuliński (301 Squadron PAF, KIA 25 September 1940), Stanisław Skalski (501 Squadron RAF), Franciszek Czajkowski (151 Squadron RAF) and Karol Pniak (32 & 257 Squadrons RAF). Czajkowski (by 151 Squadron's clerk introduced as 'Chazkowski') was wounded in combat on 31 August 1940 during his 22nd sortie during the Battle of Britain and unable to fly until 16 February 1941.

Chapter 3

Polish Battle of Britain

Flying Officer Antoni Ostowicz (1st from right) became known the first Polish pilot to claim victory during the Battle of Britain. Although the Pole reported that his wingman Pilot Officer Michael Newling was left behind, some sources claim that the latter also participated in shooting down He 111P G1+AR of 7./KG 55 on 19 July 1940 as well as Ostowicz and Flight Lieutenant Roy Dutton (1st from left). In this combat Newling's Hurricane was shot up by the German air gunner and crash-landed at Shoreham. The Pole also claimed damaging two aircraft (Do 215 on 31 July and Do 17 on 8 August) as well as the destruction of Bf 109 (also on 8 August). He was lost in action (reported missing and presumed dead) on his 38th mission on 11 August 1940 South of Swanage in Hurricane V7294, subsequently becoming the first Polish operational loss. According to German sources his body was washed ashore, however the location of his burial place is still not known.

Above left and right: A lesser known fact is that it was Pilot Officer Kazimierz Olewiński (left) to be the first Polish airman killed in Britain and during the Battle of Britain. He lost his life in a flying accident in No. 6 OTU on 29 July 1940 when his Hurricane I L1714 crashed at Walsoken near Wisbech. Olewiński previously fought in Poland with 132nd Fighter Squadron and was credited with the destruction of an enemy aircraft. If he hadn't been killed, he would certainly have participated in the Battle of Britain. His younger brother Bolesław (right) completed his training at Sutton Bridge at the time when Kazimierz lost his life. He subsequently flew in 229, 43 and 111 Squadrons during the Battle of Britain and was killed on 3 November 1940.

Opposite above left: The Polish Air Force suffered one of its non-operational losses on 9 August 1940. Wing Commander Leopold Pamuła, well known and respected flying instructor and Deputy Commander of the Pursuit Brigade, in Britain he was considered to take command of a Polish fighter squadron. Unfortunately he was unable to take up this post and he died as a result of a blood infection.

Opposite above right: 238 Squadron's 31-year-old Pole Flying Officer Michał Stęborowski, with one confirmed kill claimed three days before, he was killed in action on 11 August while flying Hurricane P3819 five miles over sea from Portland. His body was never found. *He had flown in Poland and was of a very cheerful nature* – ORB stated – *his rugged face and gentle smile are greatly missed*. Three weeks before he was accepted to join 303 Squadron.

Opposite below: During the same combat Sergeant Marian Domagała claimed the destruction of a Bf 109. He completed twenty-nine sorties during the Battle of Britain and claimed three enemy aircraft destroyed … plus one Hurricane.

Above left: Pilot Officer Dominik Fengler, former pilot of 143rd and 142nd Fighter Squadrons in Poland, for reasons unknown was posted for bomber duties to No. 301 (Polish) Squadron. He was killed on 8 August 1940 while flying Fairey Battle I L5597.

Above right: Flight Lieutenant Wilhem Pankratz in July 1940 was scheduled to command 'A' Flight of 303 Squadron. Before taking this post, however, he was killed in action while in 145 Squadron. On Monday 12 August 1940 alongside Sergeant Józef Kwieciński and Pilot Officer John Harrison he shot down Oberleutnant Siegfried Blume's Bf 110 of I./ZG2 only to become a victim of either Hauptmann Hans Karl Mayer (*Staffelkapitän*) or Unteroffizier Heinrich Rühl, both from I./JG53. Kwieciński and Harrison were also killed during this combat.

Opposite below: A Group of Polish airmen undergoing their training. Some of them joined Fighter Command and fought during the Battle of Britain. From L–R standing are: Stanisław Duszyński (2nd, 238 Squadron RAF), Antoni Łysek (3rd, 302 Squadron PAF), Józef Jeka (6th, 238 Squadron RAF), Józef Kwieciński (7th, 145 Squadron RAF), Józef Szlagowski (8th, 234 & 152 Squadron RAF). Sitting from the left are: Jan Budziński (3rd, 145 & 605 Squadron RAF) and Zygmunt Klein (4th, 234 & 152 Squadron RAF).

A group of 145 Squadron pilots at RAF Tangmere, where Flight Lieutenant Pankratz is supposed to be standing far right, hence hardly visible.

Left: Sergeant Józef Kwieciński was lost on 12 August 1940 alongside Pankratz while south of the Isle of Wight.

Below: Pilots of 32 Squadron RAF including three Poles. Pilot Officer Jan 'Fifi' Pfeiffer is standing 1st from left, Pilot Officers Karol 'Cognac' Pniak and Bolesław 'Vodka' Własnowolski are seated 2nd and 3rd from left.

Hurricane I P3981 GZ-W from 32 Squadron, was flown by Polish pilot Sergeant Wilhelm Sasak who joined this unit in September 1940.

Above left: Sergeant Wilhelm Sasak.

Above right: On 15 August 1940 the Polish Air Force suffered another loss. Pilot Officer Mieczysław Rozwadowski, former 111th Fighter Squadron pilot and Polish Campaign veteran with one shared victory prior to his last flight, was lost over Dover in 151 Squadron's Hurricane V7410.

Flying Officer Franciszek Gruszka from 65 Squadron. He was reported missing on 18 August 1940 while flying Spitfire R6713. It is believed that before he was lost he bounced one of the 8./JG3 Messerschmitts. His remains as well as pieces of his aircraft were excavated over thirty years later from Grove Marsh, Kent. No evidence of him being shot down was found.

Above and opposite below: Two photos showing Flying Officers Franciszek Gruszka, with darker hair, and Władysław Szulkowski during their time with No. 65 Squadron in August 1940. One of 65 Squadron's Spitfires can be seen in a background.

Following Gruszka's death, Flying Officer Szulkowski (2nd from right) for a while remained 65 Squadron's lone Polish 'mascot'. God only knows how his colleagues managed to pronounce his surname…

Left: . . . yet despite his limited English he was quickly adopted by the squadron's fellow pilots. Here he's pictured during a friendly hug with Flying Officer Ron Wigg.

Below: Both Spitfires of 65 Squadron were flown by the Poles. R6712 YT-N was often used by Flying Officer Szulkowski whose name was written as 'Shulkouski' and who claimed his only victory over a Bf 109 on 22 August 1940 while flying this aircraft. R6714 YT-M was also piloted by Szulkowski as well as Flying Officer Gruszka.

Gruszka's replacement was Pilot Officer Bolesław 'Ski' Drobiński, a young pilot with no combat experience, but feisty when airborne. He is seen here in Spitfire I X4820 YT-B, which he also flew after the Battle of Britain.

New Zealander Flying Officer Ron Wigg must have been fond of the Poles as here he is photographed with 'Ski' Drobiński. The latter flew five sorties during the Battle of Britain.

POLISH BATTLE OF BRITAIN

Opposite above: The same Polish pilot photographed with R6803 in which he flew in October 1940. From L–R are: Pilot Officer Norman Hancock, Flying Officer John Nicholas, Pilot Officer Bolesław Drobiński, Pilot Officer Ernest Glaser, Sergeant George Tabor and Sergeant Colin Hewlett.

Opposite below: Drobiński's identity discs made of vulcanised asbestos fibre with the cord. Both: green – octagonal in shape, and red – round, were hand stamped with the pilots name, religion (in this case Roman Catholic), service number and 'VR RAF' initials. 'Ski' wore them during the Battle of Britain.

Below: 234 Squadron RAF at St Eval with two Polish pilots: Sergeant Józef Szlagowski, who is wearing a peaked service cap and is standing 1st from right and Sergeant Zygmunt Klein, who is wearing a forage cap, and is standing 2nd from right. Both Polish NCOs still have their RAF wings without usual golden PAF eagle on their chest, worn by the Polish flying personnel during the early months in Britain. The Polish pilot's silver metal badge 'gapa' was only allowed to be worn again after General Sikorski's order dated on 7 September 1940.

Left: Both Szlagowski (pictured here) and Klein were posted to 152 Squadron, where they continued their participation in the Battle of Britain.

Below: Sergeant Szlagowski posing with the Spitfire I R6597 UM-V that was delivered to 152 Squadron right after the Battle of Britain and shot down on 28 November 1940, the same day when Szlagowski performed his only confirmed flight in this aircraft.

Pilot Officer Paweł Zenker, an experienced and battle-hardened pilot, who shared one victory over Poland, followed by two enemy aircraft claimed in Britain, was shot down on 24 August 1940 while flying 501 Squadron's Hurricane P3141 SD-W. His body was never found.

Hurricane I R4105 SD-U from 501 Squadron photographed at Gravesend, Kent in September 1940. On 18 August 1940 Pilot Officer Zenker flew this aircraft when he claimed the destruction of a Bf 109. This was most probably 5./JG53 machine flown by Hauptmann Horst Tietzen. Spitfire Ia R6800 LZ-N in the foreground was flown by Squadron Leader Rupert Leigh, who commanded No. 66 Squadron.

A group photo of 609 Squadron pilots taken at RAF Middle Wallop including two Poles: Flying Officer Piotr Ostaszewski-Ostoja (2nd from left) and Flying Officer Tadeusz Nowierski (2nd from right).

Discussion after the sortie with Ostaszewski in the middle, Nowierski (2nd from right) and Pilot Officer Janusz Żurakowski walking away.

Above: 609 Squadron pilots analysing recent action. Ostaszewski can be seen 3rd from left with Nowierski being obscured on right.

Right: Ostaszewski's surname caused a lot of hassle, so no surprise that he was called 'Osti' or 'Post'. He poses next to Spitfire I R6631 PR-Q, an aircraft that was flown by Żurakowski and Nowierski. The latter flew this mount on 24 August 1940 when it was damaged in combat.

Another photo of the same PR-Q with Pilot Officer Michael Appleby in the cockpit. Note the personal emblem under the windscreen.

Above and opposite below: Two other shots of the same R6631 PR-Q.

Right: 'Novi' Nowierski, for obvious reason by his Polish friends was called 'Łysek' (Bald Headed), was one of the Polish bomber pilots converted to fighters upon their arrival in Britain. Despite completing basic fighter pilot training he flew over Poland piloting PZL P.23 'Karaś' light bomber of 24th Light Bomber Squadron attacking German tanks. During his career in Britain he eventually rose to the rank of Group Captain commanding Nos. 1 and 2 (133) Polish Wings and also the Polish Fighters School formed within No. 58 OTU.

Although both 'Novi' and 'Osti' (standing as 1st and 2nd from left respectively) are seen here smiling, according to Nowierski they did not get on well while in No. 609 Squadron. 'It's very nice here, it's just so difficult for me to understand Ostaszewski' – wrote Nowierski about his time with 609 Squadron. Spitfire PR-L photographed here is most probably the one that Nowierski flew on four occasions in August 1940, including two operational sorties on 16th.

Spitfire I R6699 PR-L being inspected by the ground crew was flown by both Polish pilots: Flying Officers Nowierski and Ostaszewski.

The same aircraft pictured here while taxiing.

Pilot Officer Zbigniew Oleński (with a cigarette) is slightly obscured by Flying Officer John Dundas, while Flying Officer Ostaszewski, wearing a forage hat, is standing back to camera. Oleński, a pre-war test pilot, flew with 152 and 234 Squadrons RAF before being posted to 609 on 5 October 1940.

Perhaps because of the lack of common ground with 'Osti', Nowierski preferred Oleński's company?

Rather a poor quality photo that shows 609 Squadron pilots, including two Poles: 'Osti' who is standing in the middle, while 'Novi' is seated 1st from right.

609 Squadron's score board dated 13 August, 1940 when Nowierski was credited with one Bf 109 destroyed and another one damaged. Note two Ju 87s added to 'Osti's' tally, which eventually were never approved.

Oleński relaxing while at readiness…

Oleński's 1932 Pattern life-preserver proved to be popular among his RAF chums. Here Flying Officer Noel 'Aggy' Agazarian is wearing it…

Above, below and opposite below: American volunteer Pilot Officer Andrew Mamedoff is posing next to 609's Spitfire I L1082 PR-A, which he crash-landed on 24 August 1940. Eleven days earlier Nowierski flew this mount while claiming two enemy planes: one destroyed and another damaged. It was Feldwebel Hans Heinz Pfannschmidt of 5./JG53 on the receiving end. The German pilot was captured as the result of 'Novi's' action.

Above and below: L1082 was a part of a bigger bunch of Spitfires delivered to 609 Squadron straight from the production line.

L1065 PR-E was also delivered to 609 Squadron in September 1939…

The same aircraft photographed here. This Spitfire was flown by Flying Officer Ostaszewski, who, on 15 August 1940, successfully attacked a Bf 110 sharing his victory with 234 Squadron's Pilot Officer Janusz Żurakowski, who later joined 609 Squadron.

Most probably Spitfire I PR-L that was flown by Flying Officer Nowierski on 16 August. Closer inspection appears to show a mysterious emblem on the port side of its fuselage, or perhaps it's just a cloth in ground crewman's hand. However possibility of the presence of Polish AF insignia cannot be definitely ruled out.

Above and opposite below: Spitfire N3223 PR-M, here pictured before the Battle of Britain, was quite often flown by Flying Officer Ostaszewski in August and September 1940. This aircraft was lost on 5 October 1940 when his mate Nowierski participated in non-operational flight. As he couldn't lower the undercarriage he was forced to bail out and his N3223 crashed into the woods. As Pilot Officer David Crook described: 'The machine that he had been flying was not a very good one – it was rather old and slower than the new ones – so we were all very grateful to him for writing it off.'

Spitfire PR-K in the foreground, is presumably the same aircraft that, according to pilots' log books, was flown by both Nowierski and Ostaszewski on 10 August.

Above and below: Pilot Officer Zbigniew Oleński (3rd from left) is getting warm while waiting for another operation in 609 Squadron pilots' hut.

Above and below: Spitfire R6986 PR-S damaged in combat over Portland on 25 August 1940 when Flying Officer Ostaszewski was injured, preventing him from flying again until 29 August.

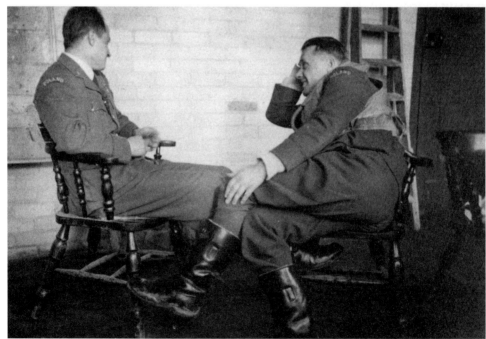

POLISH BATTLE OF BRITAIN

Opposite above: Spitfire R6986 remained with 609 Squadron until late November 1940, but before its departure it was used as a backdrop for this special photo.

Opposite below: Camera shy Pilot Officer 'Zura' Żurakowski (left) talking to his prewar Air Force Reserve Cadet Officers' School fellow- student Zbigniew Oleński.

Below left: Janusz Żurakowski ended up as a famous test pilot, gaining almost celebrity status in Canada after the war.

Below right: On 15 August 1940 Feldwebel Jakob Birndorfer's Bf 110 M8+BP of 6./ZG 76 was attacked and badly damaged by two Poles: Flying Officer Ostaszewski of 609 Squadron and Pilot Officer Żurakowski from 234 Squadron, both based at Middle Wallop. Some sources state that Birndorfer was killed when he crash-landed at North Ashey Down, Isle of Wight, while others suggest that the German pilot was shot dead by the soldiers after making a successful forced landing. Unteroffizier Max Guschewski, a radio-operator and gunner, was wounded and captured.

Above, below and previous spread: Spitfire I X4560 was delivered to 609 Squadron at the end of September 1940, becoming the personal aircraft of Pilot Officer John Bisdee (seen here climbing into the cockpit) adorned with the individual letter H as well as the pilot's family crest 'Fleur de Lis'. This aircraft was also flown twice by Pilot Officer Oleński during the Battle of Britain on 14 and 15 October, although the most remarkable 'performance' occurred on 8 November 1940 when the X4560 'burst a tyre on take-off'. Despite that surprise, the Pole continued a non-operational flight, but overturned his mount on landing when the undercarriage was caught by the soft surface of a bomb crater filled with the soil. Although the Pole remained unhurt, the aircraft was sent away for repair.

Meanwhile General Władysław Sikorski (photographed here with King George VI) put a lot of pressure on the British Government to grant independence for the Polish Air Force. On 5 August 1940 the Commander in Chief of the Polish Armed Forces and Prime Minister of the Polish Government-in-Exile agreed with his British counterpart Winston Churchill that the Polish Air Force, with its General Inspectorate, would be an integral part of the Polish Armed Forces. That was quickly followed by the legislation approved by the British Parliament on 22 August that all Polish airmen should be withdrawn from the VR RAF and subsequently join the PAF. Thereafter the PAF maintained its partial independent status remaining however under the operational and logistical command of the RAF, relying on British equipment and supplies.

Squadron Leader Adolph 'Sailor' Malan, commander of 74 Squadron photographed next to Spitfire ZP-A which was probably K9953. This aircraft was flown by Flying Officer Henryk Szczęsny in August 1940.

Both Polish pilots of 74 Squadron can be seen standing behind Malan: 'Sneezy' Szczęsny 8th from left and 'Breezy' Brzezina 10th from left and hardly visible behind his South African commander. Brzezina completed fifteen operational flights during the Battle of Britain while Szczęsny flew forty-one times.

Another group photo of 74 Squadron with Flying Officer Szczęsny being 2nd from right.

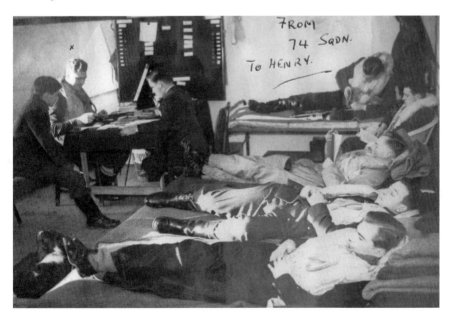

A souvenir photo for 'Henry the Pole' as Szczęsny was also nicknamed. The Polish pilot can be seen here playing cards with Flying Officer John Freeborn.

A close up picture of 'Sneezy' being preoccupied with a card game, and watched by Flying Officer Roger Boulding and dog Sam.

KG 2's Dornier Do 17Z U5+KA, which crashed at Pherbec Bridge, Barham, Kent on 13 August 1940 after being attacked by a Spitfire. Oberleutnant Heinz Schlegel's crew was captured. Flight Lieutenant Brzezina and Flying Officer Szczęsny from No. 74 Squadron claimed destruction of a Dornier each during Eastchurch and Scheerness raid.

The 13 August 1940 proved to be unlucky for Flight Lieutenant Stanisław 'Breezy' Brzezina. Although he claimed the destruction of a Do 17, followed by damaging another, he was also shot down. Here, he is visited by his good friends and fellow instructors from the Advanced Flying Fighter School. Flying Officer Marian Duryasz (left) already joined 213 Squadron RAF while Flying Officer Władysław Szulkowski (right) flew with 65 Squadron RAF. Number 13 proved to be fatal for 'Breezy' who was killed in a flying accident on 13 February 1946.

Szczęsny (left) during conversation with his fellow flying instructor from Poland, Flying Officer Marian Duryasz. The latter joined the Battle of Britain in August and flew eighty-four sorties claiming two kills, as well as the probable destruction of one enemy aircraft. Both pilots later rose to the high ranks within the PAF.

Above left: Although the identity of this aircraft is not certain, it is believed the dismantled Spitfire is Mk IIA P7361, which was flown by Flying Officer Szczęsny. The fuselage of this mount, placed on 'Queen Mary' trailer, is adorned with the PAF insignia.

Above right: Sergeant Feliks Gmur was another Polish pilot who achieved combat experience while fighting in Poland. He spent two weeks in 151 Squadron RAF before being killed in action during his sixth operational sortie over Britain on 30 August 1940, after his Hurricane R4213 DZ-I crashed at Jacks Hatch, Epping Green.

Above and below opposite below: Two Polish pilots of 501 Squadron were 'employed' in this series of publicity photos: Flying Officer Stefan Witorzeńć and Sergeant Antoni Głowacki (standing 1st and 3rd from left respectively). Note 615 Squadron's Hurricane in the background at RAF Hawkinge. These pilots flew 113 and sixty-eight sorties respectively during the Battle of Britain.

Above: Sergeant 'Toni' Glowacki seen here talking to the Intelligence Officer. We can only imagine both struggling with language as the understanding of English among the Poles was very limited by then. Note Hawker Hurricane I V7234 SD-A, which he flew on 15 August 1940 when he shot down Ju 87.

Opposite above: Two Hurricanes from No. 501 are taking off. Both of these aircraft were flown at different times by Sergeant Antoni Głowacki. He used P3208 SD-T during an operational sortie on 5 August 1940, while repeating a similar mission in the afternoon. 'Głowa' also flew this mount several times afterwards. Also Pilot Officer Franciszek Kozłowski flew this Hurricane once. P3059 SD-N was also flown on several occasions by Głowacki and for the first time on 11 August. Pilot Officer Zenker used this machine non-operationally on 12 August, before both P3059 and P3208 were shot down over Canterbury six days later with their pilots, Pilot Officer Kenneth Lee and Pilot Officer John Bland, being wounded and killed respectively.

Opposite below: The wreckage of Unteroffizier Hermann Weber's Junkers Ju 87 of 10./LG1 which is believed to have been shot down by Sergeant Głowacki. The 'Stuka' dive bomber crashed at Shorncliffe Crescent, More Hall on 15 August. On the same day the Pole damaged a Dornier. He achieved his biggest success nine days later claiming five victories in one day.

Pilot Officer Tadeusz Kawalecki fought previously in Poland as a pilot in 121st Fighter Squadron. In England, on 8 August 1940, he was posted to No. 151 Squadron and performed only two flights during the Battle of Britain. He didn't fly operationally again, but remained in the PAF as an instructor and lecturer.

Hurricane I V7434 DZ-R from 151 Squadron photographed at Digby after New Zealander Pilot Officer Irving Stanley 'Blackie' Smith, who often flew this mount, shot down one He 111 over Chapel St Leonards in Lincolnshire on 2 October 1940. This Hurricane was flown by Polish pilot Pilot Officer Gustaw Radwański on 14 September. V7434 crashed on take-off from Digby on 26 October 1940 during an evening exercise and its pilot, another New Zealander, Sergeant Douglas Stanley died of injuries the same night.

Damaged Hurricane I P3320 DZ-Y from 151 Squadron being repaired at No. 1 Civilian Repair Unit at Cowley. Flying this aircraft on 18 August 1940 Pilot Officer Franciszek Czajkowski downed a Bf 110 3U+CM from 4./ZG26 with Unteroffizier Gerhard Baar and Feldwebel Friedheim Gierga on board. This enemy aircraft was also successfully attacked by 85 Squadron's pilots.

Pilot Officer Stanisław 'Skal' Skalski finally enjoying an operational posting, seen here in the cockpit of a 501 Squadron's Hurricane

Above: 'Stanley' Skalski (1st left, 1st row) with 501's war trophy. Pilot Officer Franciszek Kozłowski, another Pole in this unit, can be seen inside pilots' hut.

Left: At the very early stage of his operational career in Britain Skalski (left) adorned his face with a moustache. Neither in Poland nor after 1940 was he seen like this. Here he is holding his pilot's log book, also known as Form 414, probably waiting for the monthly inspection by his commander.

'Skal' (far left) with a
group of 501 Squadron
pilots

While Witorzeńć (standing 2nd from right) flew with 501 Squadron since 5 August
and Skalski (sitting 3rd from right) joined this unit three weeks later, there were
other Poles attached to 'City of Gloucester' Squadron, including Sergeants
Konrad Muchowski known as 'Sergeant Konrad' and Mieczysław Marcinkowski
(sitting 1st and 2nd from left respectively). Note a metal (aluminium or lead) PAF
eagle approved for the Polish NCOs and men pinned to Muchowski's service cap.

Left: After the war Muchowski travelled to the new state of Pakistan where he served as a flying instructor. He used skills that he also gained during the Battle of Britain.

Below: Here Sergeant Konrad Muchowski (3rd from left) can be seen while in 85 Squadron with another Pole Sergeant Władysław Paleniczek (4th from right), both pictured on 5 October 1940 at Church Fenton. Paleniczek proved not to be fighter pilot material, and he was killed during a bomber mission less than a year later after joining Polish 300 Squadron.

Pilots of 253 Squadron RAF including Pilot Officer Tadeusz 'Teddy' Nowak (3rd from left)

Above left and right: Pilot Officer Janusz Maciński, photographed while in Blackpool, flew in combat in Poland as 111th Fighter Squadron pilot. After arriving in Britain, coincidently he was posted to 111 Squadron RAF. He was killed in action in the area of Folkestone on 4 September 1940 while in Hurricane II Z2309. Some sources state that he was seen bailing out. Another pilot with no grave, as he was lost in the English Channel.

Above left: Pilot Officer Walenty 'Walik' Krepski (quite often misspelled as 'Krępski' in Polish literature) of 54 Squadron RAF was lost on 7 September 1940 in Spitfire I R6901. It is believed that his death was an unfortunate result of his miscommunication in the air which was due to his poor English, hence he could not follow commands given over the R/T by his leader.

Above right: L–R are Pilot Officers Jerzy Popławski and Stefan Stegman. Both were initially posted to 111 Squadron only to be later reposted to 229 Squadron.

Opposite above: Two Poles of 56 Squadron RAF during the Battle of Britain. Pilot Officer Zbigniew Nosowicz (standing 4th from left), who is wearing the whole set of breast badges: Polish pilot's badge known as 'gapa' alongside RAF wings and PAF gold & silver braid cap eagle. Small VR brass badges are missing. On the other hand his colleague, Pilot Officer Gustaw Radwański who is kneeling 1st from right, is wearing only RAF padded King's Crown wings and VR badges. After 7 September 1940, and following General Sikorski's order and regulations, the RAF buttons were replaced by the golden Polish ones with the crowned eagle. Also the Polish ranks were added onto uniform lapels, although the RAF ranks were kept as before. It was also decided that only the Polish metal badges 'gapa' for flying personnel (they differed for pilots, navigators, air gunners etc) should be worn. The early days in Britain were quite confusing for the Poles as well as for the British.

Hurricane I N2479 US-R of 56 Squadron was flown by Flying Officer Marian Chełmecki on 7 September 1940, only three days before his departure to No. 17 Squadron. This Hurricane also flew in 213 Squadron and was transferred to No. 6 OTU before being converted into a Mk II.

Flying Officers Juliusz 'Topola' Topolnicki and Jerzy 'Jerry' Jankiewicz (1st and 4th from left respectively, although in some publications they are erroneously named otherwise) were posted to 601 'Millionaires' AAF Squadron in the middle of August 1940. Flying Officer Witold Urbanowicz also flew three times with this unit on 8 August, although he remained a 145 Squadron pilot.

Hurricane I R4120 UF-N delivered from 501 Squadron was flown once in September 1940 by each of Polish pilots: Jankiewicz on 15th and Topolnicki (who is pictured here) the following day.

Flying Officer Jerzy Jankiewicz (right) in July and August 1939 spent some time in Great Britain practising on Hawker Hurricanes due to plans to deliver some of these aircraft to Poland. He had also gained his RAF wings by then.

RAF Exeter, both Polish pilots pictured here at 601 Squadron's dispersal. Topolnicki and Jankiewicz are standing 1st and 3rd from right respectively.

Left: Flying Officer Jerzy Jankiewicz.

Below: Hawker Hurricane I R4218 UF-U with the black and white spinner (typical for 601) that was usually flown by Flying Officer Topolnicki and less frequently by Jankiewicz. The latter used R4214 quite often, especially in August 1940. Jankiewicz was wounded in action on 4 September while flying R4214.

As Jankiewicz (1st left) spent considerably more time in Britain than Topolnicki, his communication with 601 Squadron comrades was easier. This was due to coming to Britain before the war and his work in the UK on Polish Airlines' Lockheed 14, which was planned to be modified to fly to Poland as part of clandestine operations.

Flying Officer Juliusz Topolnicki claimed his only victory on 6 September 1940 shooting down Leutnant Max Himmelheber of Stab./JG2 who bailed out while his Bf 109 went down at Plum Tree Farm, Headcorn. Unfortunately the Pole shared his opponent's fate and after baling out he ended on the top of a tree at Staplehurst. He was miraculously saved from the locals, who mistook him for the German pilot, and was transported to Leeds Castle Hospital.

Most probably Flying Officer Topolnicki photographed after being rescued from the tree top.

Flying Officer Topolnicki rejoined 601 Squadron five days after being shot down, only to be killed on 21 September 1940 at 11.25 during take-off from Exeter for a formation flying exercise. His Hurricane I L1894 crashed into an anti-aircraft post and exploded. Note 87 Squadron's Hurricane in the background.

Flying Officer Jerzy Jankiewicz poses with a Hurricane (probably V6666 UF-J) with 113th Fighter Squadron emblem applied under the windscreen. Jankiewicz flew with this Warsaw based unit before the war being its deputy commander; hence it is believed that he used this motif to personalise one of 601 Squadron's Hurricanes that he used to fly during the Battle of Britain. Although Polish No. 316 Squadron formed in Britain in 1941 adopted a flying owl as their official badge, these were painted behind the cockpit,[6] not – like here – in a way how 601 Squadron pilots used to apply their personal motifs. Not to mention that Jankiewicz never flew with No. 316 and despite suggestions that there is a link between this photo and No. 316 'City of Warsaw' Squadron.

---

6. See page no. 137.

Left: Looking like a teenager, Sergeant Paweł Gallus was among the youngest Polish pilots in the Battle of Britain, although he had impressive operational experience in Poland and France.

Below: Gallus – as many ex Battle of France veterans – was rushed into 303 Squadron without appropriate conversion to Hurricanes, and after a landing accident on 12 August 1940 he was sent for further training. On 27 September he was posted to 3 Squadron at Castletown where he was accompanied by another Pole Sergeant Józef Biel (8th from left), although the latter did not fly operationally during the Battle of Britain. Here Gallus is photographed with this unit, standing 9th from left, hardly visible as obscured by his colleague.

Pilot Officer Mieczysław Gorzula (4th from left), called 'Mike' by his colleagues, came to England with no combat experience and after a short stay in 303 Squadron was reposted to 615 Squadron at Prestwick. He must have been happy there, yet a few days later he was sent to 607 and then to 229 Squadron. Gorzula rejoined 615 Squadron in December 1940.

Above left and right: It was probably Gorzula who adorned one of 615 Squadron's Hurricanes with the Polish Air Force emblem.

Above: Gorzula was not the only Polish pilot in 615 Squadron during the Battle of Britain. Interestingly Pilot Officer Bronisław Wydrowski, sitting on Gorzula's right, followed him to 607 and 229 Squadron and then also returned to 615 Squadron in December 1940.

Left: Wydrowski, wearing a 1930 Pattern flying suit, also known as a Sidcot Suit, despite being a fighter pilot in Poland, did not fly in combat, as he was posted for instructor's duty before the war.

Another example of unidentified 615 Squadron's Hurricane adorned with the PAF checker. Although Sergeant Archie Steele's connection to this aircraft is not known, Gorzula wrote that he received special permission to paint the Polish red and white insignia, hence it would be right to assume that this is 'Mike's' or Wydrowski's mount. Comparing this photo with the previous one where Gorzula is standing in the cockpit, shows that application of the PAF markings even in this unit was treated rather arbitrarily, and in this case it was done upside down. This practice can be also seen later in Polish squadrons.

POLES IN THE BATTLE OF BRITAIN

Previous page below: Sergeant Józef Jeka (left) was 22 when war broke out yet he flew several missions during the Polish Campaign. In Britain he joined No. 238 Squadron and performed thirty-one sorties during the Battle of Britain and claimed over four kills. Here he is photographed with another Battle of Britain veteran, Pilot Officer Karol Pniak. Both survived the war, but Jeka was killed when flying clandestine missions for the CIA.

Below: Mysterious Hurricane with the PAF markings used as a setting for this American volunteer pilots' souvenir photograph. From L–R are: Pilot Officer Gene Tobin, Pilot Officer Vernon Keough and Pilot Officer Andrew Mamedoff, all of whom flew during the Battle of Britain. In September 1940 three of them left 609 Squadron, where they also flew with the Poles, and joined No. 71 'Eagle' Squadron at Church Fenton, being the first three members of this new unit. As the new Polish No. 306 'City of Toruń' Squadron was forming at the same airfield, some historians speculate that the Americans used one of the Polish Hurricanes as a background. However the Poles used to apply the PAF symbol in between UZ code letters, therefore it is also right to assume that this aircraft belonged to one of the American pilots of Polish descent as many of them arrived from the USA during the war.

Above and overleaf spread: Series of photos taken by the Germans on 24 September 1940 that show Pilot Officer Witold Głowacki after his crash landing in occupied France. The former 131st Fighter Squadron pilot, who was previously shot down by the Soviets while flying an unarmed PWS-26 in 1939, initially joined No. 145 Squadron RAF before being transferred to 605 Squadron. During the Battle of Britain he flew eighteen operational sorties and claimed one Bf 110 destroyed, followed by the shared destruction of a Dornier. He also damaged a Bf 109. During the last stage of his final mission he was chased by a formation of Bf 109s, and was shot and crashed near Ambleteuse, north of Wimille near Boulogne. Although in these photos he seems to be in decent condition with only cuts to the right side of his head, he died on the same day as being transported to military hospital in Guines. Despite some historians speculating that his mysterious death could have been due to him being born in Berlin (to a Polish family living there) and therefore seen as a disgrace by the German troops, it seems to be more reasonable to believe that he died as a result of an allergic reaction to an anti-tetanus injection. Although these photos were taken after General Sikorski's dress code order being issued, Głowacki is still wearing an early form of PAF clothing: 1936 RAF uniform and wings combined with the PAF cap eagle on his left breast pocket below the button. Note also a 605 Squadron's badge on Hurricane P3832 UP-P's tail. The bear emblem was soon adopted as part of No. 306 (Polish) Squadron badge, which also consisted of a 'flying duck'. Squadron Leader Douglas Scott, its British commander, had flown with 605 Squadron before, including in the Battle of Britain, hence the presence of the bear below the duck.

Above: Flight Lieutenant Jerzy Orzechowski (10th from left), seen here with other No. 245 Squadron pilots, was quite a figure among the Poles. Former commander of 142nd Fighter Squadron and subsequently III/4 Fighter Dywizjon (Wing) in Poland, and was appointed No. 303 Squadron's commander after Squadron Leader Krasnodębski was shot down and badly wounded on 6 September 1940. However Orzechowski did not gain 303's trust and was posted to 615 and then to 607 Squadrons. He joined No. 245 while in Aldergrove and after the Battle of Britain. There are other Polish pilots in this photograph: Pilot Officer Tadeusz Koc (6th, wearing French jacket), Flying Officer Władysław Szczęśniewski (11th, right behind Orzechowski), Sergeant Stanisław Brzeski (17th), Flying Officer Jan Wiśniewski (18th) and Sergeant Bronisław Kościk (sitting on a wing). All these men were previously fighting in Poland and then posted to No. 303 Squadron where they remained undergoing training during the Battle of Britain.

Opposite above: Hawker Hurricane V6635 seen here is still without squadron markings, probably just after leaving factory. This aircraft was flown by Sergeant Michał Maciejowski of 249 Squadron during the Battle of Britain, only to be later transferred to 316 (Polish) Squadron. This plane was used to claim the first victory for No. 316 on 1 April 1941 that was shared with another Battle of Britain veteran Flying Officer Aleksander Gabszewicz.

Sergeant Michał Maciejowski is still wearing an early version of 'Poland' rectangular shoulder badges as well as RAF buttons. Initially he joined No. 111 Squadron, and then in the middle of October he was posted to No. 249 Squadron. Note his sergeant's stripes, although at that time he was in Polish lower rank of kapral. In Britain the Polish personnel were paid according to their RAF ranks, which in many cases were higher than the Polish ones. Unlike in Poland, where szeregowiecs (equivalent of AC2s) or kaprals (LACs) flew in combat, across the Channel, sergeant was the lowest rank for the flying personnel. 'Miki' Maciejowski claimed his kill when the Battle of Britain was coming to an end.

Above: The Polish contingent of No. 249 Squadron. From left are: Sergeant Stanisław Brzeski who is holding the Squadron's mascot dog 'Pipsqueak', Pilot Officer Jerzy Solak, Flying Officer Henryk Skalski and Sergeant Michał Maciejowski.

Opposite above: Another group photo of No. 249 Squadron pilots including Poles: Flying Officer Henryk Skalski (1st from right, one of three Polish fighter pilots with this surname), Pilot Officer Jerzy Solak (3rd from right), Sergeant Stanisław Brzeski (5th from right) and Sergeant Michał Maciejowski (sitting).

Opposite below: Here 'Miki' Maciejowski is photographed with his colleague Sergeant Stanisław Brzeski and the squadron's mascot. Despite his combat experience from Poland and then from France, Brzeski remained a non-operational pilot of 307 and 303 Polish Squadrons during the Battle of Britain.

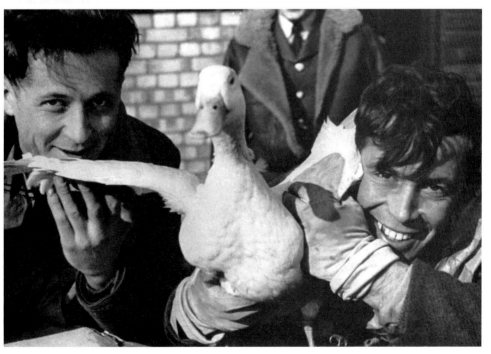

Poles of No. 249 Squadron photographed with North Weald station commander, Wing Commander Francis Beamish. Sergeant Michał Maciejowski, Sergeant Mieczysław Popek, who did not fly operationally during the Battle of Britain, and Pilot Officer Jerzy Solak, who previously was a pilot of No. 151 Squadron RAF.

The three Poles without their Irish Station Commander.

Maciejowski and Brzeski are 'hiding' on the roof of the pilots' hut.

Above, below and previous page below: Group of Polish pilots of No. 32 Squadron. Left to right: Pilot Officer Mieczysław Waszkiewicz (2nd, in Polish uniform made in France of dark blue fabric), Flying Officer Olech Kawczyński (4th, wearing Polish long flying jacket), Flying Officer Jan Falkowski (5th), Pilot Officer Wilhelm Śniechowski (6th, wearing French flying jacket) and Pilot Officer Zbigniew Janicki (7th). Only Falkowski and Janicki flew operationally during the Battle of Britain and only Falkowski survived the war. Waszkiewicz was killed on 16 April, 1941 while in 303 Squadron; Kawczyński remained in 32 Squadron to be killed on 8 May 1941; Śniechowski lost his life while in Czechoslovak 310 Squadron on 8 December 1941, and Janicki crashed in France on 13 June 1944 as 61st FS USAAF pilot.

Three experienced pilots. Left to right: Squadron Leader Witold Urbanowicz, Flying Officer Włodzimierz Łazoryk and Flying Officer Marian Pisarek. Łazoryk had to accept initial 'degradation', and despite commanding 152nd Fighter Squadron in Poland, in the Battle of Britain he flew three missions as an ordinary pilot of 615 and 607 Squadrons. In 1941 he was converted to a bomber pilot, yet later held high positions within the HQ of the PAF.

Pilot Officer Włodzimierz Samoliński was a part of small ambush unit in Poland formed within 122nd Fighter Squadron. After arriving in Britain he was posted to 253 Squadron where he gained two aerial victories before being shot down and killed over the English Channel on 26 September 1940 in Hurricane I V7470.

Above: Hurricane I P3878 YB-W of 17 Squadron was flown by Flying Officer Tadeusz Kumiega in September 1940. This aircraft was lost on 24 September 1940 shot down by Major Adolf Galland from JG26. Pilot Officer Harold Bird-Wilson bailed out and although wounded, he survived.

Opposite above: Hurricane I P2794 YB-E. Flying Officer Marian Chełmecki flew this aircraft in September 1940 although it was his lucky aircraft after the Battle of Britain when he claimed destruction of a Ju 87 and shared damage of a Do 17 on 8 and 9 November respectively. Flying Officer Tadeusz Kumiega used this Hurricane to fly in October 1940. In Flying Officer Paweł Niemiec's log book YB-E appears several times in September. Here P2794 is photographed after crashing at Monckton near Manston when Sergeant Robert Hogg was killed, only two days after the last success claimed by Chełmecki, who completed forty-one sorties during the Battle of Britain.

Opposite below left: Kumiega made his only Battle of Britain claim on 29 October 1940 after making a shared kill of a Bf 109.

Oppposite below right: Flying Officer Marian Chełmecki initially joined No. 56 Squadron and then he was posted to No. 17 Squadron. In Poland he flew operationally with the ad-hoc formed 'Instructors Fighter Flight'.

Above left: Sergeant Antoni Wójcicki of 213 Squadron RAF was a good example of a former bomber pilot who undertook fighter training in Britain. This veteran of 4th (64th) Bomber Squadron during Polish Campaign of 1939 desperately wanted to fight again. Sadly after eleven operational sorties he was killed in action near Selsey Bill on 11 September 1940 while flying Hurricane I W6667 AK-P.

Above right: The 11 September brought more losses for the Polish Air Force. No. 303 Squadron lost two of its pilots while Sergeant Stanisław Duszyński (pictured here with inscription for his sweetheart Czesława) of 238 Squadron was reported missing with his Hurricane I R2682. He only managed to fly three missions during the Battle of Britain. Note that he is wearing Polish wings with no wreath. This badge of 2nd Class pilot's specialisation was issued from 1933 and awarded to graduates of military flying schools and only after two years of active service. Airmen with lesser experience were not allowed to wear them at all. After another three years of active service, pilots were entitled for 1st Class gapa – an eagle holding a laurel wreath. Those who flew in combat had their wreaths painted in green. It is known that Duszyński was shot down over area of Romney Marsh and crashed at Little Scotney Farm. His remains, together with Hurricane pieces, were excavated in the 1970s, yet he was buried as an anonymous airman.

Opposite above: 'Cognac' Pniak was wounded in combat on 24 August 1940 as an ace while in 32 Squadron. On 16 September, after short convalescence, he voluntarily joined No. 257 Squadron. Here he is photographed with 257's pilots standing 1st from right…

…and sitting, proudly wearing Italian helmet and gaining his colleagues' attention after so called 'Spaghetti Party' on 11 November when he claimed more than one Italian BR20.

Above: Pilot Officer Franciszek Surma (right) photographed in September 1940 at RAF Tangmere where he flew with No. 607 Squadron. Flight Lieutenant Charles Bowen is wearing a German lifejacket. It would be safe to assume that it was in fact Surma's trophy from the Polish Campaign of 1939. The Pole was also known to regularly wear a German flying jacket, which nearly got him into trouble when he was shot down on 29 October 1940 while in 257 Squadron.

Opposite below: Hurricane I P2826 from Polish No. 318 'City of Gdańsk' Squadron photographed at RAF Detling in 1943. During the Battle of Britain this aircraft was flown by two Polish pilots of No. 151 Squadron. Pilot Officer Surma flew it on 2 September and Pilot Officer Solak on 20, 21 and 23 September. Note that this aircraft was converted into a Sea Hurricane fitted with arrest hook.

Pilot Officer Franciszek Surma wearing issue white aircrew frock and Pattern flying boots. Surma flew in combat over Poland claiming a shared victory of a Ju 87, which was never approved. Upon his arrival in England he was posted to No. 151 Squadron where he claimed one He 111 probably destroyed. During his stay with No. 607 Squadron the Pole added one downed Bf 109 followed by damaging a He 111, which he reported after being posted to No. 257 Squadron. The day after, on 29 October 1940, he was shot down in Hurricane P3893 and bailed out. He was killed on 8 November 1941 while in No. 308 Polish Squadron with over five kills to his credit.

Left: Sergeant Jan Budziński who flew fifty-two sorties during the Battle of Britain, firstly in 145 and then in 605 Squadron. Despite the young look, he was already an experienced pilot flying in combat over Poland with 141st Fighter Squadron.

Below: On 7 October 1940, together with Flying Officer Cyril Passy, Budziński claimed a shared destruction of an Bf 109. Unteroffizier Paul Lederer of 5./JG 27 flying an aircraft no 3665 and with a white '10' code number made a forced landing in Bedgebury Wood near Cranbrook in Kent.

Pilot Officer Stanisław Czternastek was another Polish pilot who fought in Poland. He was a member of 123rd Fighter Squadron. In Britain he was posted to No. 32 Squadron and flew two missions during the Battle of Britain. After being posted to No. 615 Squadron he was killed on 5 February 1941. He was in Hurricane I V7598 KW-S when he collided in the air with Pilot Officer Bronisław Wydrowski, who survived the accident.

Pictures of Pilot Officer Stanisław Piątkowski (sitting) taken in Britain are rare. He was the last operational Polish pilot killed during the Battle of Britain. This officer of 79 Squadron flew at least once before he was lost on 25 October 1940 during an emergency landing in Hurricane I N2708.

Above left: Sergeant Wilhelm Szafraniec in September 1940 joined 79 Squadron RAF, later being transferred to 151, 607 and finally 56 Squadrons.

Above right: Sergeant Wojciech Kloziński of 54 Squadron made two claims on 12 August 1940, but three days later he was shot down and badly wounded. Had he not suffered from injuries, he would have joined No. 303 Squadron as his post was approved.

Oppposite below: An interesting photo that shows Polish pilots enjoying their new experiences in Britain. Some of these men very soon joined operational squadrons and flew during the Battle of Britain such as Pilot Officers Janusz Maciński (111 Squadron, killed during his 5th mission, 1st from left in 3rd row), Ludwik Martel (54 and 603 Squadrons, 2nd from left in 3rd row) and Stefan Kleczkowski (302 Squadron, 3rd from left in 2nd row). Pilot Officer Czesław Gauze (1st from left in 2nd row) and Czesław Tarkowski (seated) both joined No. 85 Squadron on 1 October 1940 before being posted to 605 Squadron twenty-three days later. Unfortunately they remained non-operational pilots during the Battle of Britain. Tarkowski was shot down on 6 November and bailed out from 29,000ft (!), but luckily survived; sadly Gauze lost his life only eleven days later. They were both victims of JG26 pilots.

Sergeant Szymon Kita (middle), a former co-operation unit pilot, flew with 85 and then with 253 Squadrons. He noted a few claims in his flying log book during the Battle of Britain, but none of these were ever accepted.

Above left: Pilot Officer Józef Gil, 43 Squadron.

Above right: Pilot Officer Edmund Jereczek, 43 & 229 Squadrons.

Above and opposite below: Two pictures of No. 85 Squadron Hurricanes most probably photographed on 18 October 1940 when Pilot Officer Tarkowski flew aircraft V7240 VY-M. This Hurricane is visible in both pictures flying third from left and second from right respectively.

Meanwhile many more Poles flew operationally during the Battle of Britain in RAF squadrons. Most of them were very experienced pilots yet they only managed to fly once or twice. They were: Flying Officer Bernard Groszewski, 43 Squadron.

Above left: Sergeant Bronisław Malinowski, 43 Squadron.

Above right: Sergeant Włodzimierz Mudry, 79 Squadron.

Above left: Pilot Officer Aleksander Narucki, 607 Squadron.

Above right: Sergeant Antoni Seredyn, 32 Squadron.

Chapter 4

Polish Squadrons Entering the Battle

302 'City of Poznań' Squadron

Series of pictures taken on 7 August 1940 when General Sikorski visited RAF Leconfield and inspected No. 302 Polish 'City of Poznań' Squadron which had been stationed there since the early days of July. The Polish Commander in Chief was accompanied by (among others) Inspector General of the PAF Air Vice Marshal Stanisław Ujejski and Inspector General of the RAF Air Marshal William Mitchell. Note that some of the airmen are still wearing darker uniforms made in France, including Squadron Leader Mümler, the oldest Polish Battle of Britain pilot, born in 1899. Funnily enough, although the semi-independent status of the PAF had been approved by then, yet there was still some kind of rivalry between the Poles who had recently arrived after fighting in France and those who came to Britain during the winter of 1939 and spring 1940. The latter, more settled ones, were called 'those from RAF' by the new arrivals.

Above: Sikorski decorates some of the pilots who had previously fought in France with the Cross of Valour. These men were: Flight Lieutenant Piotr Łaguna, Pilot Officers Tadeusz Czerwiński, Julian 'Roch' Kowalski, Włodzimierz Karwowski, Czesław Główczyński and Sergeant Antoni Markiewicz. Except Karwowski, they were all former GC 1/145 pilots, with Łaguna being its deputy commander and then commander. This French chapter certainly influenced No. 302 Squadron's badge, consisting of a raven that showed the link to the former fighter units of Poznań's 3rd Air Regiment, which was painted over the French national colours with the number of 1/145 on top of the diamond shaped background. As photos of 302 Squadron aircraft from this period are extremely rare, it is shame that only a wingtip of one of the Hurricanes is visible here…

Opposite: … but there it is! Hurricane WX-K, almost certainly V6569, is being passed by a cameraman. The PAF emblem is yet to be applied. This aircraft was regularly flown by Flight Lieutenant James Thomson as well as Pilot Officer Stanisław Łapka. The latter shared destruction of a Do 17 on 15 September 1940 before being shot down, both in V6569.

Above: Flight Lieutenant Piotr Łaguna, Polish A Flight Commander, reports to General Sikorski.

Opposite above: Despite the initial plan to gather a large number of randomly chosen pilots, most of whom never joined No. 302 Squadron, the core list was finally determined. Kazimierz Niedźwiecki was initially appointed its first commander, yet after his tragic accident in No. 6 OTU, it was Squadron Leader Mieczysław Mümler who took this post. Juliusz Frey and Tadeusz Opulski were chosen to be Flight Commanders yet again they did not join No. 302. Instead, Frey was posted to 607 Squadron RAF while Opulski was transferred to twin 303 Squadron. Only the Polish personnel of the first PAF fighter squadron formed on British soil pose in this photo, with their national emblem of the crowned eagle. Some of the airmen are still in the uniforms they were wearing when they came from France.

Opposite below: Another souvenir photo taken during the Battle of Britain. Now the non-Polish members joined and are posing together. Squadron Leaders William Satchell and Mieczysław Mümler known as 'King of the Castle' are sitting side by side in the middle. Flight Lieutenant James Farmer's white dog 'Peggy' did not get Polish approval from the beginning. Perhaps because this breed was not common or popular in Poland?

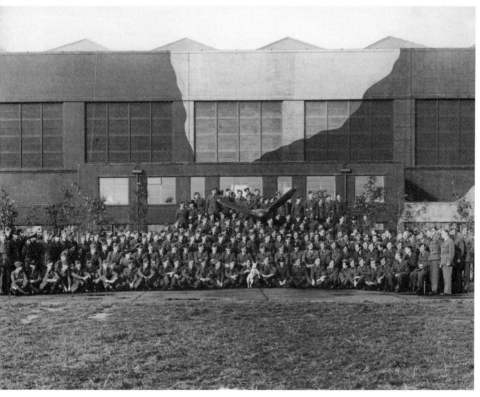

Above: Squadron Leader William 'Jack' Satchell was the British counterpart of Mümler, despite that, the latter had huge leading and fighting experience as Dywizjon (equivalent of RAF Wing) Commander in Poznań, and with over four kills into his account. Meanwhile Satchell, who was a ground controller in France and then crashed a 141 Squadron's Defiant prior to Battle of Britain and had no operational experience at all, was rather critical of Mümler's methods. This led to disagreements and finally to the removal of the Polish commander.

Opposite below: From the left: Pilot Officer Władysław Gnyś (2nd), Sergeant Antoni Beda (4th) and Pilot Officer Stanisław Chałupa (5th), all three went into the Battle of Britain with experience gained during the Polish and then French Campaign. Gnyś became famous as the first (double) victor of the Second World War who also added one and one shared victory in France. Beda, here still wearing a French flying jacket, claimed more than one victory as GC I/2 pilot, while Chałupa shared unconfirmed victory over Polish skies and then added more than two kills in France. The other two pilots: Pilot Officer Marceli Neyder (1st) and Sergeant Marian Rytka (3rd) since 25 and 17 October 1940 respectively were in 303 Squadron undergoing training, with the latter joining No. 302 on 23 October.

On the other hand there was a 41-year-old officer, who not only flew in combat on numerous occasions, but who also knew most of his pilots well, many of whom flew operationally in Poland and in France with more than twenty-seven kills between them.

Pilot Officer Czesław Głowczyński's luck ran out on 17 August 1940 when his Hurricane I P3927 WX-E caught fire while airborne and the Pole force landed in flames at Weel, 5 miles south of Leconfield, suffering extensive burns. He was pulled out from the wreckage by the local baker and later photographed in Beverley Hospital, where it was initially intended to amputate his left leg. Only the quick intervention of Flight Lieutenant Tadeusz Chłopik, who pretended to be a family member, saved the future flying and operational career of this experienced flier.

Another souvenir photo taken during the Battle of Britain showing 302 Squadron pilots. From left to right standing are: Pilot Officers Bronisław Bernaś, Władysław Gnyś, Stanisław Łapka, Edward Pilch (both Łapka and Pilch were the first two Polish pilots to be posted to 302 Squadron), Wacław Król, Flight Lieutenant Jan Czerny, Sergeant Antoni Beda, Pilot Officer Jan Maliński, Sergeants Antoni Łysek, Wilhelm Kosarz, Marian Wędzik, Pilot Officer Aleksy Żukowski, Sergeant Antoni Markiewicz, Pilot Officers Stanisław Chałupa, Zbigniew Wróblewski (wearing Polish uniform made in France), Sergeant Eugeniusz Nowakiewicz, Pilot Officer Włodzimierz Karwowski and Sergeants Zbigniew Kleniewski (non-operational pilot) and Jerzy Załuski. Sitting from left are: Pilot Officer Jerzy Czerniak (another pilot wearing Polish uniform), Flight Lieutenant Franciszek Jastrzębski, Flying Officer Peter Carter, Flight Lieutenants James Farmer, James Thomson, Piotr Łaguna, Squadron Leaders William Satchell, Mieczysław Mümler, Flight Lieutenant William Riley, Pilot Officers Julian Kowalski, Tadeusz Czerwiński and Flight Lieutenant Antoni Wczelik, who is also wearing Polish uniform. Shortage of RAF uniforms should not be surprising as the majority of 302 Squadron pilots only recently arrived from France. Hence a very strict order was issued on 22 August 1940 forbidding those leaving the base from wearing French uniforms that were not known to the British civilians. Pilot Officers Stefan Kleczkowski and Stefan Wapniarek are missing from this photo.

Three non-Polish officers of No. 302 Squadron, from left: Flight Lieutenant James Farmer, who was in charge of aerial training, Flying Officer Hutchings, Education Officer and Flight Lieutenant James Thomson, A Flight Commander.

A group of 302 Squadron pilots with Flying Officer Marian Pisarek from No. 303 Squadron in the middle (4th from left, the only one with the Polish pilot's badge). The others are: Pilot Officers Władysław Kamiński, Jerzy Czerniak, Włodzimierz Karwowski, Pisarek, Stanisław Łapka, Julian Kowalski, Jan Maliński and Flight Lieutenant Piotr Łaguna.

Right: Flight Lieutenant James Farmer's aerial training methods were not popular with the Polish pilots.

Below: Pilot Officer Stefan Wapniarek, Jan Maliński and Sergeant Eugeniusz Nowakiewicz. The latter had nearly four confirmed kills from France and added one Ju 88 probably destroyed during the Battle of Britain. This happened during the disastrous mission on 18 October 1940 when four pilots, including Wapniarek, lost their lives.

Hurricane V6744 WX-C arrived in 302 Squadron in September 1940. On 15 October it was flown in combat by Pilot Officer Zbigniew Wróblewski. Three days later, during a fatal and almost disastrous mission, Pilot Officer Włodzimierz Karwowski flew it, attacking a Bf 109 without success and then safely returning to Northolt. On 26 October Flight Lieutenant Thomson flew it on an operational sortie. One of 302 Battle of Britain veterans, Flying Officer Julian Kowalski, damaged a Ju 88 on 4 March 1941, flying this aircraft and making his first claim since the Battle.

POLISH SQUADRONS ENTERING THE BATTLE

Opposite below: Flying Officer Paul Harding who joined No. 302 Squadron as an Intelligence Officer, interrogates Pilot Officer Łapka, who for obvious reasons was nicknamed 'Mały' (Little). It was rather an easy-going task for Harding as he spent some time in Poland before the outbreak of war, working for a Warsaw-based soap manufacturer where he picked up some words. Despite that, he struggled with some technical terms, this did not prevent him from being an unofficial translator. With or without his contribution, finally the manuals were translated into Polish and apart from being used within 302 Squadron, copies were also delivered to other Polish fighter units such as 303, 306 or 308. The other pilots in this photo are Sergeants Marian Rytka (1st), Eugeniusz Nowakiewicz (3rd), Julian Kowalski (5th) and Jan Maliński (6th).

Below: Pilots of 302 Squadron. From left to right are: Sergeant Nowakiewicz, Pilot Officer Karwowski, Flight Lieutenant Łaguna, Pilot Officer Maliński and Pilot Officer Władysław Kamiński. The latter, unlike his colleagues, is already wearing Polish pilot's badge. Maybe this is because he joined 302 Squadron after the Battle of Britain, previously undergoing training in No. 303 Squadron.

Above, opposite and overleaf: Series of photographs that document the last seconds of the crew as well as what was left of Do 17 from 1./KG76. This aircraft with the code letters F1+FH and serial number 2361 with Oberleutnant Robert Zehbe (pilot), Unteroffizier Leo Hammermeister, Obergefreiter Ludwik Armbruster, Unteroffizier Hans Goschenhofer and Unteroffizier Gustav Hubel was shot down and crashed on 15 September 1940 at Buckingham Palace Road. The last two crew members were killed while the pilot died later from his wounds, presumably as a result of being beaten by furious civilians. It is believed that it was Pilot Officer Stanisław Chałupa of No. 302's Green Section who was involved in this loss as he claimed one Dornier destroyed and another probably destroyed. He also later described in details the encounter and final moments of the German crew. There were also British and Czechoslovak pilots attacking the same bomber, which was finished off by colliding with Sergeant Raymond Holmes of 504 Squadron.

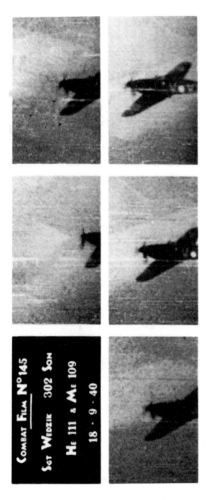

A gun camera footage from Sergeant Marian Wędzik's Hurricane from Yellow Section taken on 18 September 1940 shows another No. 302 aircraft with the PAF symbol under the cockpit and individual 'W' letter, most probably flown at that time by Pilot Officer Stefan Wapniarek of Blue Section. First letter of 302's code 'WX' is also visible. Although some authors claim that Wapniarek flew P3924 WX-Y that day, the analysis of this photo suggests otherwise. The latter claimed one Ju 88 destroyed followed by four other Ju 88s reported to be shot down by his colleagues as well as two Dorniers. Also two Do 17s and one Ju 88 were probably shot down, as well as one more Ju 88 known to be damaged. Wędzik, apart from catching an image of his colleague, chased two Ju 88:s 3Z+AS Werk Nr 3147 and 3Z+BS Werk Nr 3142 both of 8./KG77 and reported one of them as destroyed, although there is strong belief that he was also involved in the destruction of the second one. Interestingly there was an aviation journalist of Polish sounding name Unteroffizier Alfred Smolarczyk on board of 3Z+AS, who was killed.

Above: The wreckage of Ju 88 3Z+GH from 1./KG77. This enemy aircraft was initially and unsuccessfully attacked on 19 September 1940 from 700 yards by Flight Lieutenant William Riley, who was 302's B Flight Commander. It was Flying Officer Julian Kowalski, who followed with his attack from 250 closing to 50 yards to make sure that his action is deadly. This Ju 88 crashed in Culford, 4 miles north-east of Brandon and very close to the local school's playground, killing Unteroffizier Paul Dorawa, Gefreiter Erich Schulz and Gefreiter Heinz Scholz. Only Unteroffizier Ernst Etzold bailed out and survived.

Opposite above: Three of 302 Squadron pilots, from the left: Pilot Officers Marceli Neyder, Wacław Król (also known as Black Wacek due to his dark hair, or 'Monarch' as his surname translates as 'King') and Bronisław Bernaś. Out of these three officers only Król had previous combat experience. He fought in Poland with some success, and was shot down on 5 September 1939. He also led 121st Fighter Squadron during the later stage of fighting. In France he was posted to GCII/7 where he claimed two aerial victories and two other e/a as probably destroyed. He also claimed one Bf 109 during the Battle of Britain on 15 October.

Opposite below: Flight Lieutenant Franciszek Jastrzębski had the rather unusual nickname of 'Agnes'. Despite this, he was a natural born fighter and leader. Former Commander of 132nd Fighter Squadron and with three kills confirmed, he was given command of the B Flight of 302 Squadron. On 15 September 1940 he shared victory of a Do 17, adding the probable destruction of another bomber of the same type three days later. He was lost over the Channel on 25 October while in Hurricane I V7593 WX-V.

Above: Although this picture was taken after the Battle of Britain, it shows Hurricane I V6865 WX-L that was flown by 302 Squadron pilots in October. Squadron Leader Satchell claimed one Bf 109 probably destroyed on 26 October flying this mount. Interestingly an individual letter 'L' became almost a permanent code for 302's commanders during the forthcoming years.

Opposite above: Another strong character of 302 Squadron. Flight Lieutenant Tadeusz Chłopik, photographed while in No. 1 Air Force Training Centre where he served as a well-respected flying instructor. Note a PWS-18 trainer aircraft manufactured in Poland under British Avro Tutor licence in the background. Although he made two claims on 15 September 1940 Chłopik was also killed, being the first 302 Squadron pilot lost in action. Even though he bailed out from his Hurricane I P2954 WX-E, he was found dead after his parachute failed to open. Some time ago the replica of his aircraft was used as the gate guardian at the entrance to the Imperial War Museum in Duxford.

Opposite below: A souvenir photo of 302's Battle of Britain pilots with a member of the ground crew. It is often forgotten that without the sacrifice made by the fitters, armourers and electricians, the Battle of Britain could not have been won. Chief of Polish mechanics Sergeant Wacław Oyrzanowski (2nd from left) wrote his personal diary that was published in Poland many years after the war, and allows us to understand 302 Squadron's situation in 1940. Sadly he died of wounds following a flying accident in 1943, when he joined a Mosquito pilot for a test flight. The others in this photo are: Pilot Officers Jan Maliński (1st), Zbigniew Wróblewski (3rd), Stanisław Łapka (4th) and Flying Officer Julian Kowalski (5th).

136

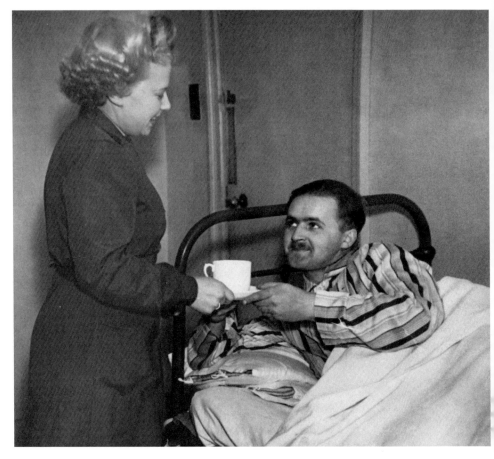

Above: Pilot Officer Stanisław Łapka of Yellow Section of 302 Squadron didn't have time to enjoy his success of victory over a Dornier 17 which he shared with Sergeant Antoni Siudak on 15 September 1940 as he was shot down and bailed out from his Hurricane I V6569 WX-K. He broke his leg on landing and was treated in Ely Hospital before being transferred to Newquay Hospital on 8 October.

Opposite above: Hawker Hurricane I V6735 photographed at RAF Pembrey in spring 1941 while in No. 316 (Polish) Squadron. This aircraft was delivered to No. 302 Squadron in October 1940, coded WX-M and flew its first operational sortie on 12 October with Pilot Officer Carter inside. Five days later Pilot Officer Kleczkowski crash-landed in Sittingbourne, ending V6735's second operational mission and its short Battle of Britain career.

Opposite below: Flying Officer Peter Carter was killed on 18 October 1940.

POLES IN THE BATTLE OF BRITAIN

Above and opposite above: The 18 October 1940 remains the worst day in 302 Squadron's history, when four pilots, including three Poles, were killed. B Flight flew home after the combat in extremely bad weather conditions when a series of tragic accidents occurred. Pilot Officer Stefan Wapniarek was killed during an emergency landing in Hurricane I P3827 WX-R at Nutwood Farm near Cobham. He tried to avoid colliding with Flight Lieutenant Thomson's aircraft. Flying Officers Jan Borowski (P3930 WX-X), who only joined the squadron the previous day, and Peter Carter (P3931 WX-V) crashed at Kempton Racecourses in Sunbury, both losing their lives. Pilot Officer Aleksy Żukowski (V6571 WX-Q), who also flew operationally for the first time in Britain, made a fatal attempt to land at Harp Farm near Detling. The last two Poles were experienced combat pilots gaining their fighting acquaintance over Poland and then over France. This was a really sad time for the 302 Squadron as only the day before, Sergeant Jerzy Załuski overturned his Hurricane V7417 WX-T after an emergency landing and broke his neck, while Pilot Officer Stefan Kleczkowski crash-landed near Sittingbourne in V6735 WX-M. Both pictures show the very few items that were found after Borowski's death, including partially burnt French ID Card and his watch that stopped at 4.34 pm when the pilot was killed.

Post Battle of Britain photo of Hawker Hurricane V6753 WX-Z that was delivered to 302 Squadron in October 1940. Note application code letters typical for 302 Squadron.

Above and opposite: Three photos that seem to have a very little connection to the Battle of Britain as they show Sergeant Mieczysław Popek's landing mishap on 19 August 1941. This 303 Squadron pilot crash-landed dangerously close to the railway line in Speke. The aircraft P3932 RF-C shown here was in fact a Battle of Britain veteran, used by 302 Squadron as WX-C since August 1940. It was flown operationally by Pilot Officer Łapka, Sergeant Palak, Squadron Leader Mümler and Flying Officer Kowalski. The last entry in 302's Operations Record Book can be found under 14 September when Kowalski was scrambled and flew uneventful afternoon patrol. P3932 in September 1940 was replaced by V6744 and delivered to Polish No. 306 Squadron. Later it was also used by 256 Squadron before being transferred to Polish No. 315 Squadron and finally to 303 Squadron, where its flying career was sealed. Note Sergeant Henryk Starzyński, chief mechanic, wearing Polish leather coat, supervising recovery action.

Day after the Battle. Sir Archibald Sinclair, Secretary of State for Air, visited Northolt on 1 November being accompanied by General Sikorski, here obscured by Sinclair. From right are 302 Squadron pilots: Pilot Officers Stanisław Chałupa, Władysław Gnyś, who talks to distinguished guest, being watched by Edward Pilch and Flying Officer Tadeusz Czerwiński.

303 'Tadeusz Kościuszko, City of Warsaw' Squadron

Above: Great photo of No. 303 Polish Squadron personnel illustrating variety of uniforms used at this early stage. Flying Officer Walerian Żak (1st from left) is wearing a Polish 1936 uniform with armlets that was made in France as well as Flight Lieutenant Jarosław Giejsztoft (Polish Intelligence Officer, 4th) who is similarly dressed in a pre-war pattern light grey uniform. These men were part of a significant group which only recently crossed the Channel. As flying personnel were so valuable for Fighter Command it was decided to send them directly to participate in operations as there was no time for practicing in OTUs. It was assumed that their flying skills were up to date, yet flying Hurricanes proved to be more complicated than Moranes, Dewoitines or Blochs. Unsurprisingly some of the Poles had to go for further training. Flying Officer Marian Pisarek is standing 2nd, and Pilot Officer Hughes (Education Officer) is 3rd.

Opposite: Squadron Leader Zdzisław Krasnodębski (left) took command of 303 Squadron. It was an obvious choice as the former commander of both: 111th Fighter Squadron (that was 303 Squadron's predecessor) and then subsequently III/1 Fighter Wing, he knew most of the former Warsaw's 1st Air Regiment pilots, who admired his leading skills. Flight Lieutenant Tadeusz Opulski (he led 112th Fighter Squadron in Poland) was initially appointed 303's B Flight Commander, and in this picture, similarly to Krasnodębski, he is wearing the Polish uniform and ranks.

Above left: Sergeant Karol Krawczyński, former 112th Fighter Squadron pilot, who fought in Poland and in France under Opulski's command, joined No. 303 Squadron with the first group. However, he was diagnosed with fighting exhaustion and was unable to continue operational duties.

Above right: Sergeant Stefan Wójtowicz also arrived from France, yet very quickly learnt his first English words of 'Me Polish pilot – I love you.' These words did their magic rather efficiently because here he is, photographed with his sweetheart Ruth Nicholson. She was left in tears soon after this picture was taken.

Opposite: This man was definitely needed and remained busy by helping with communication between the Poles and RAF personnel. Interpreter Pilot Officer Joseph Walters (left) with Flight Lieutenant Opulski. The latter did not fly operationally during the Battle of Britain remaining as 'non-effective, sick'. Opulski subsequently volunteered for Bomber Command and was killed in 1943 in a flying accident.

Initially Opulski was replaced by Flight Lieutenant Stanisław Pietraszkiewicz. 'Petro', as he was known to his pilots, remained a non-operational pilot of 303 Squadron and on 9 September 1940 was appointed to command Polish 307 Night Fighter Squadron. He was posted back to 303 Squadron in late October, but in January 1941 he took command of No. 315 (Polish) Squadron (where this photo was taken). It was Flying Officer Ludwik Paszkiewicz who took command of 303's B Flight. The Hawker Hurricane PK-O pictured here is in fact V7538 that was used during the Battle of Britain by 249 Squadron.

POLISH SQUADRONS ENTERING THE BATTLE

Opposite below: Two Poles in their Polish style uniforms: Polish Adjutant Flight Lieutenant Witold Żyborski (left) and Pilot Officer Jan Zumbach with RAF's Intelligence Officer Pilot Officer Edward Hadwen. Żyborski's son Andrzej was 303 Squadron's driver during the Battle of Britain. After completing fighter pilot training, he later flew with No. 306 Squadron.

Below: Flight Lieutenants Athol Forbes and Canadian John Kent from RAF – B and A Flight Commanders respectively, with Pilot Officer Hughes.

POLISH SQUADRONS ENTERING THE BATTLE

Opposite above: A moment of relaxing before another 'scramble' for Squadron Leader Krasnodębski, who led No. 303 Squadron until 6 September 1940 when he was shot down and badly burnt.

Opposite below: Photos of 'King' wearing flying gear are rare as the Polish commander flew only five operational sorties between 1 and 6 September. Note his Polish-French uniform with shoulder ranks.

Below: All these 303 pilots fought over Poland and in France. After arriving in Britain, apart from struggling with the language, they had to adapt to the Imperial measuring system to be able to assess the distance and height. The whole cockpit drill was very much different to what they had learnt across the Channel. From left are: Sergeant Stanisław Karubin (wearing Polish and RAF wings alongside the pre-war style ribbon of Polish Cross of Valour, Flying Officer Wojciech Januszewicz (in French uniform), Pilot Officer Mirosław Feríc, Sergeant Stefan Wójtowicz and Sergeant Eugeniusz Szaposznikow.

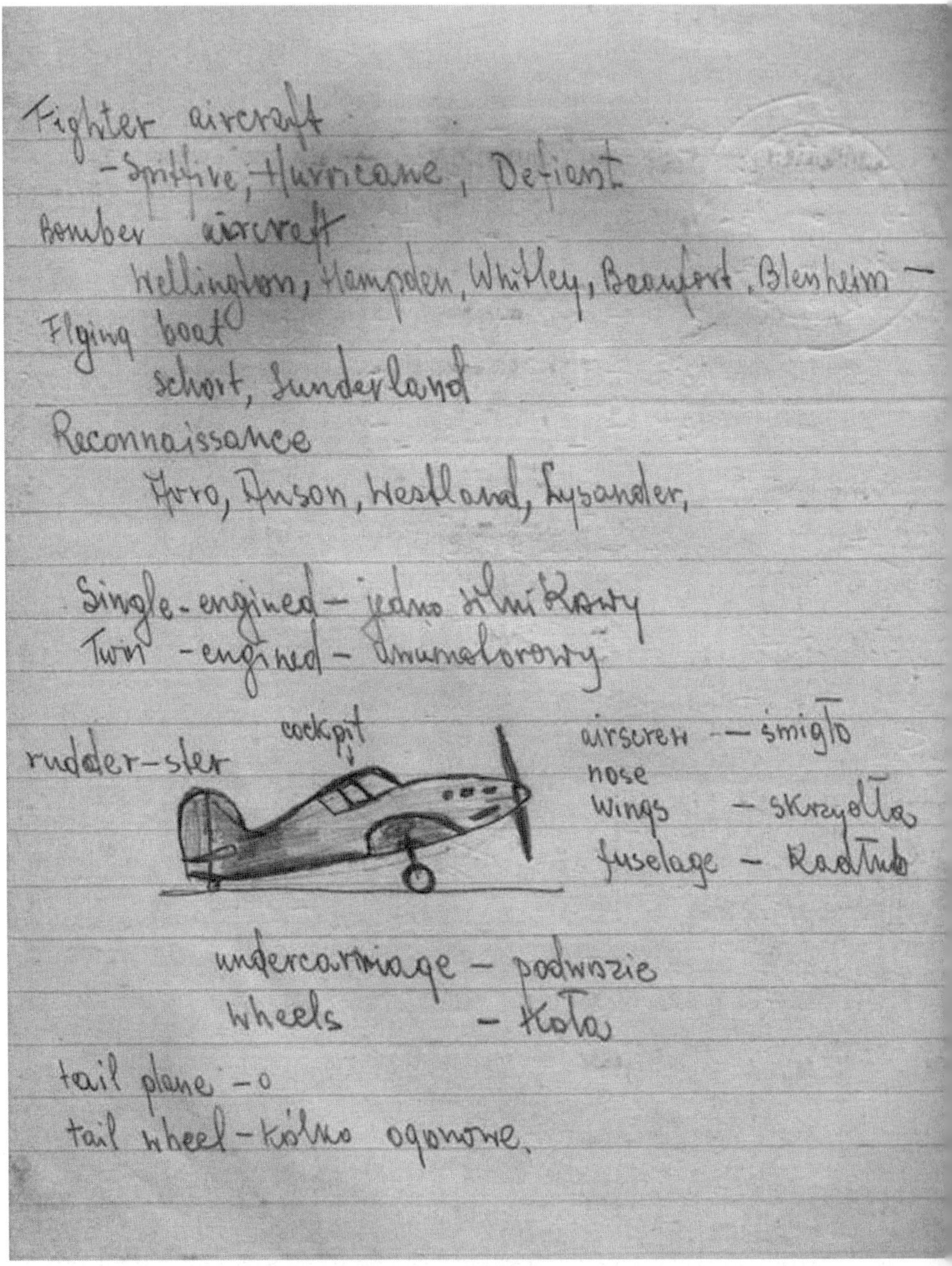

Fighter aircraft
- Spitfire, Hurricane, Defiant
Bomber aircraft
Wellington, Hampden, Whitley, Beaufort, Blenheim —
Flying boat
Short, Sunderland
Reconnaissance
Avro, Anson, Westland, Lysander,

Single-engined — jedno silnikowy
Twin-engined — dwumotorowy

rudder — ster   cockpit   airscrew — śmigło
                                         nose
                                         wings   — skrzydła
                                         fuselage — kadłub

undercarriage — podwozie
wheels   — koła

tail plane — o
tail wheel — kółko ogonowe,

First steps in English can be seen here, written in Flying Officer Wacław Łapkowski's diary: airscrew – śmigło, wings – skrzydła, fuselage – kadłub…

152

Right: 303's commander from AAF, Squadron Leader Ronald Gustave Kellett, initially did not get 'approval' from his Polish subordinates, as in their eyes he was only a 'Sunday flier' with no combat experience.

Below: The first victor for 303 Squadron Flying Officer Ludwik Paszkiewicz (note his Polish ranks) talks to Pilot Officer Hadwen. Although 303 Squadron had previously flown few operational sorties, Paszkiewicz's claim made on 30 August 1940 officially started the unit's days of glory.

Above, below and opposite: What was left of a Messerschmitt Bf 110C Wn 3615 M8 + MM photographed at the Barley Bins Farm, Kimpton. This aircraft from the 4th Staffel ZG 76 was attacked by Flying Officer Paszkiewicz on 30 August. Its pilot Oberfeldwebel Georg Anthony was killed while Unteroffizier Heinrich Nordmeier, radio operator and rear gunner, managed to bale out. Nordmeier, pictured here, was found wounded. In one of these photos the Home Guard members are holding up a bullet-damaged section of M8+MM's wingtip. The second attacker was Pilot Officer Bryan Wicks of No. 56 Squadron.

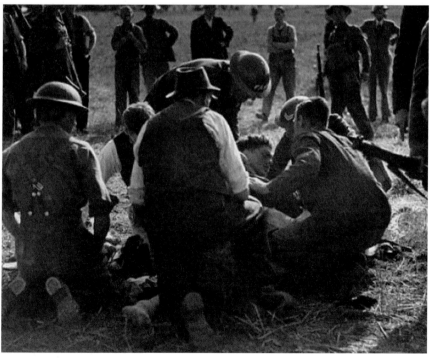

Pilots and ground crews of No. 303 Squadron presenting various fashion elements typical of the transition period in 1940. From the left are: Sergeants Jan Kowalski, Josef František, Marian Bełc, Flying Officer Ludwik Paszkiewicz (wearing French flying jacket), Sergeant Józef Mikołajczak (mechanic), Sergeant Mirosław Wojciechowski (wearing 1933 Pattern flying gauntlets) and three unidentified mechanics. Bełc lost consciousness and crash-landed on 8 August 1940 and was subsequently diagnosed with icterus which prevented him from operational flying until 18 September, 1940.

POLISH SQUADRONS ENTERING THE BATTLE

Opposite below: Dispersal hut slightly damaged on landing by Hurricane I R4178 RF-G on 31 August 1940, piloted by Squadron Leader Kellett. British commander brought down one Bf 109 that day, while Flying Officer Henneberg, Pilot Officer Ferić, Sergeants Karubin, Szaposznikow and Wünsche each claimed one Bf 109.

Below: Jan Zumbach did not fly operationally in Poland as he had a landing mishap in PZL P.11c on 26 May 1939 when he collided with a car and suffered from a complicated leg fracture. On 7 September 1940 he claimed his double kill that led to his total score of seven confirmed victories during the Battle of Britain, none of them in Hurricane I P3975 RF-U seen in this picture. Note the 'Kościuszko' emblem under the cockpit. During August and September 1940 the squadron badge was applied in two different locations: like here – under the cockpit and behind the canopy. It is often believed that these different locations for the emblem were used to differentiate between the A and B flights, yet there are photos which contradict this thesis. This aircraft is one of three Hurricanes with an individual 'U' letter that were used by 303 Squadron during the Battle of Britain. P3975 was flown by Sergeant František when he shot down two enemy aircraft on 2 and 3 September, then on 5 September Sergeant Karubin shot up two Bf 109s with it. This Hurricane was damaged in combat on 7 September when Pilot Officer Witold Łokuciewski claimed one Dornier destroyed and another one as probably destroyed. On 9 September it was again František who scored a double victory while flying P3975, which was shot up and crash-landed. Four days later this Hurricane was replaced by V6673 and on 15 September Sergeant Wojciechowski claimed Unteroffizier Streibing's Bf 109 E-7 of 1./LG2, one more Bf 109 and shared the victory of a Dornier while flying this aircraft.

P3975 was back in 303 to allow Wojciechowski to destroy one Bf 109 on 17 September, only to be replaced one more time, when V7503 arrived. The latter was a successful machine for two pilots: Sergeant Bełc claimed one Bf 109 on 26 September, Flying Officer Marian Pisarek two Bf 110s, including one probably destroyed on 5 October and one Bf 109 a day after. Note different location of the squadron emblem which is not fully applied.

Above: An unidentified Hurricane during maintenance.

Opposite above: Another unidentified Hurricane, probably P3700 RF-E. Flying Officer Henneberg, who is sitting inside the cockpit, receiving technical updates from a crew member dressed in Polish leather jacket. This pilot flew P3700 only once on 8 September on an early patrol with no contact with the enemy, one day before this mount was lost.

P3700 RF-E is taking off from Northolt. Note 'Kościuszko' emblem applied typically for the A Flight of 303 Squadron during early days of September 1940. Its replacement had it painted behind the cockpit.

POLISH SQUADRONS ENTERING THE BATTLE

Opposite above: The same aircraft, pictured here, is being prepared for another mission by LAC Ryszard Kwiatkowski. Pilot Officer Mirosław Ferić flew this mount on 6 September when he was credited with one Bf 109. Three days later Sergeant Kazimierz Wünsche was shot down and badly wounded while flying this aircraft, which crashed at Saddlescombe Farm.

Opposite below: Sergeant Stanisław Karubin is climbing into P3700's cockpit. Two ground-crew members standing in front are: LACs Mieczysław Kowalski and Jerzy Waluga. Interestingly, Kowalski's grandson is currently serving at RAF Northolt.

Below: The same pilot and the same aircraft photographed with AC1 Antoni Rossochacki who was mortally wounded in the bombing of Leconfield on 27 October and died on 5 November becoming the Battle of Britain's only non-flying loss of 303 Squadron.

POLISH SQUADRONS ENTERING THE BATTLE

Opposite above: Close up of the same aircraft P3700 while being refuelled.

Opposite below: The replacement for P3700 with an individual letter 'E' already applied. It is occasionally said that this aircraft P3901, which was often flown by Pilot Officer Jan Zumbach and then quite regularly by Squadron Leader Witold Urbanowicz, had the Urbanowicz's motto: 'We do not beg for freedom, we fight for it', painted on its fuselage. However Urbanowicz said once it was in fact RF-A adorned with this slogan. 'Cobra', as he was known to his colleagues, made nine of his claims in P3901.

Below: P3901 had been used by numerous pilots throughout the Battle of Britain and only in January 1941 was it replaced by V6757. Apart from Urbanowicz the other Polish pilot who made claims in it was Sergeant Karubin for a Bf 109.

P3901 was also the only known 303 Squadron's Hurricane adorned with personal motif of cartoon creature, which is the only one personalisation mark known so far. Donald Duck became a personal trademark of Jan Zumbach (and few of his consecutive aircraft), who was also nicknamed after famous Disney's character. Lack of 'We do not beg for freedom…' could be interpreted both ways: those words were never there or were only temporarily applied, possibly in chalk.

Opposite below: A mysterious lithography of a Hurricane RF-A that Witold Urbanowicz used as a letterhead after the war when he was writing to his veteran-colleagues. The picture was made by Max Graces of Max&Rex in the USA, yet its origins are not certain: was it only the artist's imagination supported by Urbanowicz's memory, or had he seen and copied an original photo? Not only does this aircraft have a PAF checker (probably artificially added or poorly enhanced) under its cockpit which, if real, could be reminder of P3120 being flown by 302 Squadron before, but according to Urbanowicz this was the one adorned with, 'We do not beg for freedom…', a patriotic slogan that he learnt from his freedom fighter grandfather. Why would Urbanowicz request to personalise an aircraft that he only flew twice in operations?

Above and above right: Another unidentified Hurricane is getting ready.

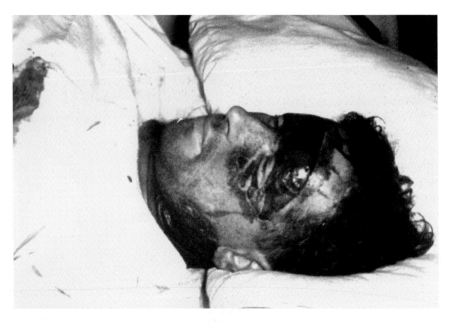

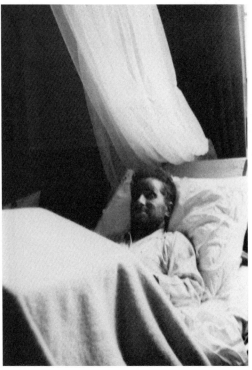

Above, left and opposite: Series of photos showing Squadron Leader Zdzisław Krasnodębski, called by his pilots 'The King', taken in hospital after being shot down in P3974 RF-J on 6 September 1940. He was badly burnt and never returned to operational flying, becoming a member of 'The Guinea Pig Club'.

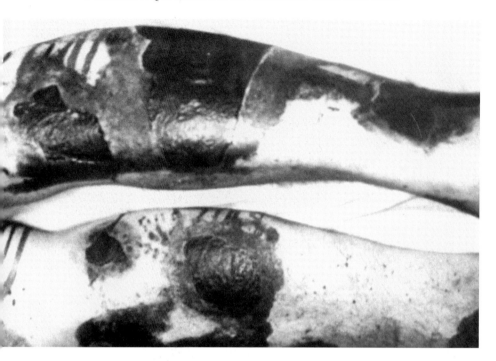

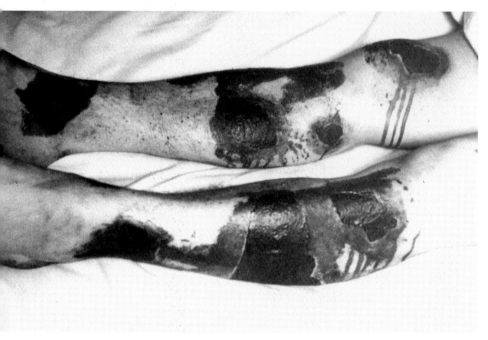

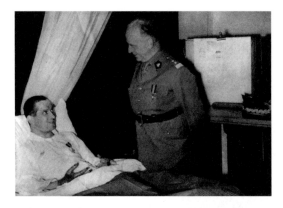

On 5 October 1940 Krasnodębski looked much better, hence he was visited by General Sikorski who decorated him with the Silver Cross of Virtuti Militari.

Acting Squadron Leader Urbanowicz, who took command of No. 303 Squadron, is posing in front of P3120 RF-A obscuring the middle part of the aircraft. This and two following photos show the application of a red diagonal stripe on the rear fuselage, which was required by Fighter Command from 18 September 1940 for easy identification from below. Flying Officer Zdzisław Henneberg scored one Do 17 and one Bf 109 on 15 September, and Flying Officer Grzeszczak scored one He 111 on 26 September flying this Hurricane. P3120 was delivered to Northolt on 6 September and stayed there exactly a month, previously being flown in 302 Squadron as WX-W, so it is quite possible that this aircraft was adorned with a PAF checker. Known 302 Squadron pilots who flew this machine were Pilot Officers Carter, Chałupa and Wapniarek.

Above and below: Both photos of Hurricane V6665 RF-J show application of a quick identification band distinguishing friendly or foe aircraft. This aircraft was flown by several pilots and a few of them made claims with it: Sergeant Michał Brzezowski shot down two He 111s on 11 September, followed by another destroyed on 26 September by Sergeant Tadeusz Andruszków. The latter was shot down and killed the very next day in this mount.

Three ground-crew members posing with V6665 before this aircraft was lost in action.

Hurricane N2661 RF-J was V6665's replacement, which remained in 303 Squadron until the end of 1940.

Above and below: Battle-damaged Hurricane R4175 RF-R without 'Kościuszko' badge being inspected by the ground crew on 5 September 1940. This was the replacement for P3645 RF-R, which was damaged by Flying Officer Paszkiewicz during initial familiarisation. Flying R4175 Sergeant František scored a double victory on that day. This pilot also made further claims on 6, 26 and 27 September in this aircraft. Sadly, he was killed on 8 October 1940 in a flying accident while in R4175.

Above: Hurricane I V7235 RF-M, with 'Kościuszko' badge still under the cockpit, could be easily called Ludwik Paszkiewicz's personal mount as the Polish pilot scored five out of his six kills flying this aeroplane between 7 and 26 September. This Hurricane survived the Battle of Britain, but its usual pilot was killed the day after his last victory. On 5 October Sergeant Bełc claimed one Bf 109 flying this Hurricane. Three of Polish mechanics pictured here: Tadeusz Żurakowski (1st), Antoni Majcherczyk (3rd) and Lech Dzierzbicki (4th) later joined PAF's flying personnel and none survived the war.

Opposite above: Pilot Officer Jan Zumbach photographed with Warrant Officer Kazimierz Mozół. The latter was popular especially among 111th Fighter Squadron veterans, where he also played the same vital role as chief mechanic. The aircraft in the background is V7244 RF-C.

Above, previous page below and opposite: A series of photos of the same V7244 being maintained by 303's mechanics. The 303 badge is slightly obscured. This aircraft was flown extensively by various pilots but survived the Battle of Britain. Numerous claims were made by its Polish pilots. Sergeant Kazimierz Wünsche reported one Bf 109 downed on 31 August, also Flying Officer Bohdan Grzeszczak destroyed one Bf 109 on 27 September. But it was Sergeant Eugeniusz Szaposznikow who shot down seven enemy aircraft out of his eight kills in Britain flying this Hurricane. He also damaged one Bf 109 in it.

A group photo of 303 Squadron pilots standing from left: Sergeants Josef František (although he voluntarily joined the PAF in the summer of 1939 and had his RAF service number from the Polish batch, he is proudly wearing a Czechoslovak pilot's badge), Jan Kowalski, Mirosław Wojciechowski, Flying Officer Ludwik 'Paszka' Paszkiewicz, Sergeant Marian 'Doctor' Bełc and Flying Officer Walerian 'Auntie' Żak. Apart from František of course, who was a foreigner in this group, both Bełc and Wojciechowski were an addition to this assemblage of ex-1st Air Regiment veterans, back in Poland both serving in 152nd and 142nd Fighter Squadrons respectively.

Sergeant Tadeusz Andruszków (3rd from left) was ex-162nd Fighter Squadron pilot (therefore another non-1st Air Regiment flier in 303 Squadron) with combat experience and the second youngest Polish pilot that fought in the Battle of Britain. He was still 19 years of age when he was killed in action in Hurricane V6665 RF-J on 27 September 1940. Flight Sergeant G. Quirk from the RAF and Flying Officer Wacław Wiórkiewicz, Technical Officer, are standing 5th and 6th respectively.

Above, below and opposite above: A series of photos that show 303 Squadron pilots relaxing and awaiting another sortie. From left: Flying Officers Paszkiewicz, Żak and Pilot Officer Łokuciewski.

Now Flight Lieutenant John Kent, A Flight Commander, joined them. Initially rather sceptical about flying with Poles, he soon gained their trust and nickname of 'Kentowski' or 'Kentoffski' (the Polish way of saying 'he's one of us').

Above: First from left Pilot Officer Jan Daszewski, also called 'Long Joe', is showing the hint of a tan. On 7 September 1940 he was shot down and badly wounded and only rejoined his unit a year later. He is being watched by 'Paszka' Paszkiewicz, while Pilot Officer 'Tolo' Łokuciewski and Flying Officer Wacław Łapkowski are seated 4th and 5th. Łapkowski, also known as 'Foka' (Seal) was shot down two days after Daszewski's misfortune and spent several months away with wounds and burns. Neither survived the war, both were lost in action in 1942 and 1941 respectively. Sergeant Wojciechowski is standing behind.

Opposite above: František's R4175 RF-R and Paszkiewicz's V7235 RF-M at Northolt. The second Hurricane has 'Kościuszko' emblem reapplied behind the cockpit. V7235 was damaged by František on 8 August when he landed with the undercarriage up. Despite some rumours, with no evidence, that the Czechoslovak pilot successfully fought in France claiming numerous victories, it would be right to assume that his only previous flying experience was in his native country and in Poland, where he only flew biplanes with fixed undercarriages. Interestingly, his French Carnet Individuel (log book) confirms only ten flying hours in Escadre d'Instruction (Training Flight) based in Aulnat, mainly in obsolete Dewoitine D.500s. František is also known to have worked together with ground crew in France.

Above and previous below: Two photos of V7284 RF-A getting ready for combat. Interestingly this aircraft was flown by Squadron Leader Ronald Kellett on 5 September when he was shot up and emergency landed at Biggin Hill. V7284 was replaced by P3120.

Opposite and overleaf spread: Five interesting photos of a Hurricat P3544 LU-V that between 16 and 26 September 1940, still as a Hurricane, was used by 303 Squadron and coded RF-H. This aircraft was flown by A/Squadron Leader Urbanowicz, Pilot Officer Ferić, Sergeants Andruszków and Szaposznikow and eventually Flying Officer Wojciech Januszewicz. It was the latter who flew P3544 during its final mission when the Hurricane sustained severe damage and its pilot had to immediately land near Fareham. After conversion to Catapult Aircraft, on 6 November 1941 this aircraft flew as Hurricat or Catfighter, as both names were used, operating from CAM ship. In May and June 1942 it was flown by Battle of Britain veteran, Pilot Officer John 'Tim' Elkington.

Hurricane I L1696 during aerodynamics trial. This aircraft arrived in 303 Squadron in the middle of September 1940 and was marked as RF-T only to be lost on 27 September with Flying Officer Paszkiewicz in its cockpit. The Polish B Flight Commander was shot down and killed in Borough Green.

Right: Although the Poles called him 'Psotny Dyzio' (Enfant Terrible), Squadron Leader Kellett tried his best to get them on board. Here he is photographed with one of the strongest characters – Jan Zumbach.

Below: The British commander could speak French, which definitely helped him to communicate with the Poles. From left are: Flying Officer Zbigniew Wysiekierski (Photo Reconnaissance Unit pilot visiting his colleagues), Kellett, Flying Officer Hadwen and Flying Officer Henneberg, while Sergeant Karubin is standing in the hut door.

Opposite: Kellett's main opponent. Witold Urbanowicz was known for his strong and uncompromising opinions; the Pole often criticised his British counterpart, yet both maintained civilised partnership for the sake of 303 Squadron's safety and readiness.

Below: The same group is seen here entering pilots' hut. Interestingly, Pilot Officer Zumbach is carrying a FN 1910 handgun in a leather holster. Although RAF officers were issued with Webley revolvers or Colt automatic pistols during the Battle of Britain, in most cases they flew without them. Zumbach, known for his adventurous character, probably decided to have extra protection (that he presumably brought from Poland or France) in case of being shot down over the enemy territory. He 'recalled' that he had it and threw it away on 15 September 1940 after an emergency landing in a minefield and surrounded by British troops, although this didn't actually happen…. That is the kind of larger-than-life person he was!

Kellett's 'Three Musketeers', as he used to describe Sergeants Wünsche, Karubin and Szaposznikow, who very often looked after his back. 'As the weeks went by I knew I could rely on their abilities and loyalty,' Kellett said. The last two are informally wearing both Polish and RAF wings, together with pre-war ribbons of Cross of Valour granted to them in France.

Very often incorrectly called a 'guest' in 303 Squadron and surrounded by myths of his claims in France, yet Sergeant František was one of several Czechoslovak airmen who officially joined the Polish Military Aviation in 1939. He even flew reconnaissance missions during the Polish Campaign. Despite having an opportunity to go back and to fly with his countrymen in 1940, and after an argument with a Czechoslovak officer, he remained in the PAF. He learnt Polish yet maintained his national pride, respected for his patriotism by the Poles. Here, he's photographed with Hurricane V7289 RF-S, flying in which he made three claims on 11 September. This Hurricane was also flown by Sergeant Wünsche, who scored two Bf 109s destroyed and one probably destroyed on 5 and 6 September. Three weeks later Flying Officer Żak was shot down in this aircraft over Leatherhead, suffering from serious wounds which eliminated him from flying for a long time. The day before, however, he shot down one He 111 and damaged another flying V7289.

191

POLISH SQUADRONS ENTERING THE BATTLE

Opposite above: The well-known Polish writer and adventurer, Arkady Fiedler, who visited 303 Squadron in Northolt, wrote about František describing him as 'a throwing lava volcano'. The temperament of the Czechoslovak pilot was demonstrated in full scale after being shot up in combat on 9 September by Hauptmann Mayer of Stab I./JG53 or Leutnant Götz from JG54 and crash landing in Hurricane P3975 RF-U in a cabbage field of Cambridge Farm near Brighton. He spent the following evening in one of Brighton's pubs terrorising customers eventually being, not without a fight, incapacitated and arrested by Constable Geoffrey Wren. After spending the rest of the night at the local police station, the following morning and still with a hangover, František shook hands with the Bobbies saying, in his poor English, 'no hard feelings', and left for Northolt.

Opposite below: Despite Polish ground crews tirelessly working hard, there was a constant shortage of aircraft as they kept returning with battle damage or were destroyed in combat. Therefore, Hurricanes from neighbouring 1 RCAF Squadron were borrowed to keep No. 303 operating. P5180 YO-R was flown by Flight Lieutenant Kent on 6 September and only barely returned to Northolt when the engine caught fire.

Below: Another aircraft from No. 1 RCAF Squadron that was flown on 7 September by Flying Officer Zdzisław Henneberg. Despite Hurricane V6605 YO-N being damaged in combat, its Polish pilot brought it back home claiming two victories (including one e/a probably destroyed).

11 September 1940 saw Group Captain Stefan Pawlikowski's visit to Northolt. This experienced pilot flew during the Great War and commanded the Pursuit Brigade during the Polish Campaign in 1939 hence he knew many 303 Squadron pilots and ground crew. Here he is photographed during casual discussion with the unit's personnel. From left standing are Pilot Officer Witold Łokuciewski, Flying Officer Zygmunt Wodecki (Medical Officer who is still wearing Polish uniform made in France), Sergeant Josef František, Flying Officer Ludwik Paszkiewicz and Pilot Officer Joseph Walters (interpreter). Seated are Acting Squadron Leader Witold Urbanowicz (still in RAF VR uniform), Group Captain Pawlikowski (hardly visible) and Flight Lieutenant John Kent.

A puzzling picture of the pilots' hut door adorned with a 'Winged Salamander' emblem? Not anymore! It is well known that No. 303 Squadron inherited the badge of former 111th Fighter Squadron. This included a peasant's hat and two scythes that symbolised Tadeusz Kościuszko Uprising against Imperial Russia in 1794, combined with the elements of the American flag as Kościuszko later fought for American Independence. The original badge was created by one of the American volunteer pilots who fought against Bolshevik Russia in 7th Squadron (great predecessor of 303 Squadron). However, No. 303 consisted equally of pilots from two former Fighter Squadrons from Warsaw: 111th (Krasnodębski, Cebrzyński, Henneberg, Januszewicz, Urbanowicz, Ferić, Palusiński, Zumbach, Karubin, Szaposznikow, Wünsche, Wójtowicz) and 112th (Opulski, Łapkowski, Paszkiewicz, Żak, Daszewski, Łokuciewski, Kowalski, Krawczyński,[7] Siudak). The later unit had its origins in 19th Squadron that was also sent to fight against the Bolsheviks in 1919 and 1920 and, as it is believed, used a 'Flying Salamander' as their badge. After receiving new PZL P.7 fighter planes, a new badge of a 'Fighting Cockerel' was introduced by 112th Squadron, and in the first half of 1939, the unit's PZL P.11s were still adorned with it. Presumably in August, in anticipation of war, the new camouflage and tactical numbers were applied as well as the 'Winged Salamander' badge being reintroduced. Not only did 303's B Flight unofficially use it during the Battle of Britain to show their origins and rivalry with ex-111th Squadron colleagues, but probably they managed to impress Group Captain Pawlikowski, a 19th Squadron veteran, during his visit to Northolt.

---

7. Karol Krawczyński did not fly operationally during the Battle of Britain.

Above: Pawlikowski talks to the ground crew. Note that Urbanowicz is still wearing Flying Officer's stripes. When he was given command of 303 Squadron 'Kobra' had Polish rank of porucznik, which is equivalent of Flying Officer.

Opposite above: Polish Liaison Officer with Fighter Command inspects one of the six Hurricanes delivered to 303 Squadron on 7 September. This machine P3939 was previously used in 302 Squadron, hence the presence of the PAF checkerboard which is turned around 90°. Since its application had been allowed in June 1940 and approved on 5 August 1940 by the British, this symbol was consequently used by 'City of Poznań' Squadron. This is the only photograph known to date of 303 Squadron's Hurricane adorned with the PAF emblem. Apart from this, the earliest known photo of 303's aircraft with the Polish marking was taken on 20 January 1942! In the case of this Hurricane it was decided to keep an individual 'H' code letter, although on the port side it was reapplied typically for 303 Squadron: the original 'H' was overpainted with the 'RF' squadron code letters, while a new 'H' was painted between the RAF roundel and the tail, so opposite to how it was in 302. The latter used a mirror effect application on both sides.

This code letters change is more visible here, where an old, overpainted 'H' is still noticeable. On the same day that Pawlikowski visited Northolt, Flying Officer Henneberg reported the destruction of a Bf 109 and He 111 while flying this P3939 RF-H.

Hurricane P3939 remained with 303 Squadron for only eight days. Interestingly Sergeant Wójtowicz claimed two Dorniers destroyed on the same day this Hurricane was delivered to Northolt, making its debut. On 15 September 1940 Sergeant Andruszków bailed out from this aircraft over Dartford, after sharing victory of a Dornier 17 and sealing P3939's fate.

Opposite above: Sergeant Michał Brzezowski (1st from right) was the youngest Polish pilot to participate in Battle of Britain. Here he is helping Sergeant Szaposznikow with a 1932 Pattern life preserver and C-2 single point, quick release seat parachute.

Opposite below: The same pilots photographed at dispersal, joined by Sergeant Stefan Wójtowicz, who is standing in the middle. He was to be killed on 11 September while Brzezowski (1st left) outlived him by only four days.

Hurricane I V7242 RF-B inspected by Warrant Officer Kazimierz Mozół, who stands on its port side under the watchful eye of Flight Lieutenant Witold Żyborski, Polish Adjutant. Sergeant Szaposznikow was credited with the destruction of a Bf 109 on 31 August while flying this aircraft. This was followed by Flying Officer Urbanowicz's claim of one Bf 110 on 6 September being his first kill since joining 303 Squadron. Next day, Pilot Officer Zumbach claimed two Dorniers with this aircraft. On 11 September Sergeant Wójtowicz flew V7242 for the last time and was seen by the locals fighting a lone battle and shooting down one Bf 109 while a second one was assumed to be probably destroyed. A single bullet went into his cockpit and the Pole was killed by shrapnel, crashing into Hoggtrough Hill near Westerham.

Flight Lieutenant Jarosław Giejsztoft, who is wearing a French leather jacket and service cap with Polish rank, is holding a letter from Westerham Fire Brigade that describes the last moments of Wójtowicz's combat and his death. It is believed that the Polish pilot shot down Unteroffizier Albert Heckmeier of I./LG2 whose aircraft crashed at Wrotham Hill, he possibly fought with another Bf 109 that crash-landed at Wissant.

RAF issue map that was found with Wójtowicz's body.

Above, below and previous page: Funeral of two Polish pilots killed in action on 11 September as Sergeant Wójtowicz's death was not the only loss for 303 Squadron. Flying Officer Arsen Cebrzyński, veteran of campaigns in Poland and France, was killed during his first operational sortie over Pembury while flying Hurricane I V6667 RF-K. Note Sergeant Karubin is still wearing a long Polish flying jacket while Pilot Officer Ferić and Sergeant Bełc are wearing French jackets.

Above: Another example of Hurricane I with an interesting history. Early series L2099 arrived in 303 Squadron on the same day when this unit suffered its first fatal casualties. Although this aircraft is obscured by the ground crew, its individual letter 'O' is partially visible. Several pilots claimed victories flying it: Pilot Officer Łokuciewski claimed one Do 17 and a Bf 109 the same day L2099 was delivered. Four days later Flying Officer Żak scored another Dornier, but returned in damaged aircraft. On 27 September Flight Lieutenant Forbes added one Ju 88, while Sergeant František claimed the destruction of one Bf 109 and probably shooting down another Bf 109 on 30 September. Finally, Sergeant Bełc downed Unteroffizier Bley of 4./LG2 on 7 October. L2099 remained in 303 Squadron until 23 December. This aircraft has an upright rod-type aerial mast that in the summer of 1940, and in later models, was replaced with streamlined tapered ones. Also radio equipment had been updated from TR9 HF fitted in early models to T/R Type 1133 VHF.

Above, below and previous page below: On 18 September 1940 General Władysław Sikorski, Polish Commander in Chief and Prime Minister, visited Northolt to see how his already famous boys were coping with their daily duties. Note the Polish national flag. From June 1940 a Polish Air Force 1930 flag (white and red flag with Polish eagle and checkerboard) was allowed on the mast below the RAF flag on a regular basis. Only in 1944 was it decided that the Polish AF flag should be next to the RAF one whenever there was a Polish Station Commanding Officer present.

Sikorski arrived with General Stanisław Ujejski, Inspector General of the PAF, who can be seen on his right.

Both commanders of 303 Squadron (in the middle, back to camera with Mk. II steel helmets and gas masks that were compulsory during official events) seem to be on good terms, at least during the General's visit.

Above: Sikorski talks to Kellett. As he is only assisted by Ujejski here, it would be right to believe that he communicates with Kellett in French, the language that the latter knew from his French mother.

Opposite above: Sikorski's trip to Northolt had more purpose than just pure courtesy. He was there to decorate some of the pilots who fought bravely during the Battle of Britain with the Silver Cross of Virtuti Militari and some others with the Cross of Valour. There was very little time between approval and execution, as the awarding decision was also made in September. For example Urbanowicz requested the VM for his predecessor on 12 September, stating that Krasnodębski continued 'commanding' his unit, or rather advising his men, even while in a critical state in hospital!

Opposite below: Decorated men from left: Flying Officers Henneberg, Paszkiewicz, Urbanowicz (obscured), Pilot Officer Ferić, Flying Officer Januszewicz, Pilot Officers Łokuciewski (being decorated by the General), Zumbach, Sergeants František, Szaposznikow, Flying Officer Pisarek. Note that Henneberg and Paszkiewicz are wearing two stars of porucznik (Lieutenant) on their lapels, Ferić, Łokuciewski and Zumbach have their Polish podporucznik (Sub Lieutenant) stars, while Szaposznikow is 'ignorantly' wearing the correctly positioned, yet no longer needed, RAF wings alongside his Polish 'gapa', despite Sikorski's order dated eleven days before! Other pilots not captured here, who received their VMs were Squadron Leader Krasnodębski, Flying Officer Łapkowski, Pilot Officer Daszewski (all three in hospital), Sergeant Karubin and Sergeant Wünsche. Sergeant Wójtowicz was posthumously awarded the VM.

Above: Sergeant František being decorated by Sikorski. Note the absence of 'Poland' shoulder badges on his uniform. Despite one well known portrait photo of this Czechoslovak ace where 'Polands' were artificially yet poorly applied, there is no evidence of him wearing them. Interestingly his name was Polonised, often appearing as 'Józef Franciszek'. Flying Officer Pisarek, who is looking at the General, is also wearing the Polish Lieutenant's two stars lapel badges. On the same occasion some of the Polish airmen were decorated with the Cross of Valour: Flying Officer Wodecki (Medical Officer) who is standing alone 1st from right wearing RAF Doctor's lapel badges alongside the larger Polish equivalent from France, as another recipient, Sergeant Rogowski, was in hospital, while Flying Officer Cebrzyński and Sergeant Brzezowski were posthumously awarded with the Cross of Valour.

Opposite and overleaf above: Hawker Hurricane I V7504 RF-G with longer, pointed Rotol propeller hub and glare shield ahead of the cockpit, was the only known 303 Squadron Hurricane with such modifications at that time. The two other photos show that the propeller hub had been replaced. Note serial number that is overlapping with the letter 'R'. This aircraft arrived by the end of September and on 30 September was flown by Sergeant Karubin, who destroyed the Bf 109 of Unteroffizier Vogl from 4./JG53. On 5 October Squadron Leader Kellett used this Hurricane to damage another Bf 109.

210

POLISH SQUADRONS ENTERING THE BATTLE

Opposite below: Thursday, 26 September 1940, around 2pm; pilots of 303 Squadron lined up to welcome King George VI. From left to right are: A/Squadron Leader Urbanowicz, Squadron Leader Kellett, Flying Officers Hughes, Paszkiewicz, Henneberg, Januszewicz, Grzeszczak, Pilot Officers Zumbach, Ferić, Palusiński (?), Flying Officer Wiórkiewicz, Sergeants Kowalski, Bełc, Andruszków and Szaposznikow.

Below: In this photo Urbanowicz went behind first line while Flying Officer David Upton (RAF Adjutant) is standing in front and holding 303 Squadron's Chronicle, which started in 1939 as Mirosław Ferić's personal diary and slowly evolved as the squadron's official document. The story goes that it was Ferić who approached the King asking for his signature, but his English was very basic at that time and so Upton came to the rescue. Despite being extremely tired, the Polish pilots look relaxed and calm. Unfortunately, both Flying Officer Paszkiewicz (2nd from left, smiling to photographer) and Sergeant Andruszków (12th) would be killed in action the very next day.

Above: Men of 303 Squadron waiting for the Royal arrival.

Opposite above: Casual-looking conversation. From the left are A/Squadron Leader Urbanowicz, His Majesty King George VI, Squadron Leader Kellett, Air Vice Marshal Keith Park CO of 11 Group and Group Captain Stanley Vincent, Northolt station commander. Interestingly, the latter was not initially impressed with the Poles claiming their kills and he wrote: 'Every day produced staggering figures of successes against the enemy, and I was frankly, dubious as to the accuracy of the claims for a short time, but after accompanying the Squadron in a Hurricane two or three times I saw what was happening and knew that claims were genuine without any doubt whatever.' Note one of A Flight's Hurricanes still with 303 Squadron badge applied below the cockpit, visible in the background.

Opposite below: The King reads the list of 303 Squadron victories. Both commanders of 303 Squadron are dressed in flying gear as they were scheduled for flying duties that day. Urbanowicz performed a lone patrol before the King's arrival. Two hours later both commanders flew from Northolt with the rest of squadron and Urbanowicz shot down an He 111 while Kellett downed a Bf 109.

214

Above: Flying Officer Upton is still patiently awaiting the monarch's attention with the 303 Squadron Chronicle under his arm.

Opposite above: The King had shaken hands with Urbanowicz, now he talks to Flight Lieutenant Forbes with Flying Officers Paszkiewicz and Żak awaiting their turn. In less than two hours they would shoot down one He 111 and one He 111 plus another damaged respectively. For both, these would be their last victories during the Battle of Britain as they were shot down on 27 September with Paszkiewicz being killed and Żak seriously wounded. Forbes claimed one He 111 on 26 September returning from combat in damaged V7465 RF-V.

216

Here the King shakes hands with Flying Officer Henneberg, who is wearing recently introduced combination of Polish and RAF ranks, who was also off duty that day. Flying Officer Januszewicz is next with Flying Officer Grzeszczak, Pilot Officer Zumbach (still in Polish/French uniform) and Ferić waiting. Januszewicz had to force land after combat in P3544 RF-H later in the afternoon while Grzeszczak reported one He 111 destroyed despite his Hurricane P3120 RF-A being damaged. Zumbach had a double score of one He 111 and one Bf 109. Ferić was not operational that day.

POLISH SQUADRONS ENTERING THE BATTLE

Opposite above: Pilot Officer 'Ox' Ferić is being introduced to the King. This interesting photo shows inconsistency in dressing code typical for that period, but also for this man. Here Ferić is wearing faultless RAF uniform with Pilot Officer's stripes while well-known group photography and a series of photos taken in late September and October respectively show him back in a Polish uniform.

Opposite below: Historical moment. His Majesty signs 303's Chronicle...

Below: ...and walks off. Some historians claim that the King left Northolt right after this inspection, asking to be informed about results of the combat. In fact the King stayed at the station and talked to the pilots upon their return from the operation when he learned that 303 Squadron destroyed thirteen enemy aircraft without loss, although four Hurricanes were damaged.

Above: Farewell to the King. 'I gave the signal to off caps and say "God save the King"' – Kellett wrote. 'Certainly a loyal shout resulted but what it meant I shall never know.'

Opposite: Two pieces of the temporary certificate of Silver Cross of Virtuti Militari that Flying Officer Paszkiewicz was decorated with only nine days before they were found with his burnt body at Crowhurst Farm, Borough Green on 27 September 1940. Here, someone has completed the missing text.

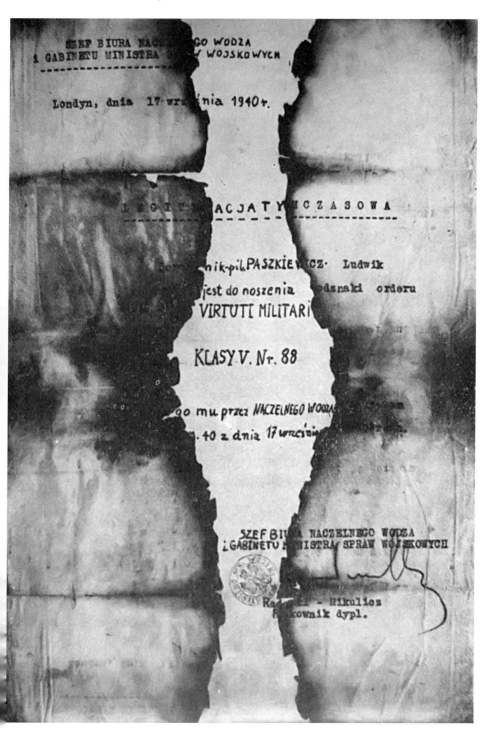

Above and opposite: On the same day Pilot Officer Ferić claimed two kills: Bf 109 and He 111, yet no losses of any Heinkel in that area and that time are known. Some historians, however, believe that his victim was a Ju 88A 3Z+HK from 2./ KG 77. This aircraft, which as the author believes, was in fact fired at by Sergeant František, went down and crashed at South Holmwood. The whole crew bailed out but Unteroffizier Wilhelm Menningmann did not survive. Here, Junkers' pilot Unteroffizier Rudolf Schumann photographed shortly after being captured. There were other 303 pilots claiming 'He 111' during the morning encounter on 27 September, while Luftwaffe lost three of KG 77's Junkers in combat.

Above and below: Another farewell. This time to close friends. Flying Officer Paszkiewicz and Sergeant Andruszków were shot down and killed in Hurricanes L1696 RF-T and V6665 RF-J respectively. Pilots' bodies are being taken from Northolt chapel on 2 October. After the loss of 'Paszka', Flying Officer Pisarek took command of B Flight.

Both coffins being transported to the nearby Northwood Cemetery with Flying Officer Giejsztoft, A/Squadron Leader Urbanowicz and Flying Officer Januszewicz (on the opposite side of the lorry) being a guard of honour. Januszewicz would be killed in action three days later.

Paszkiewicz's coffin being carried to his resting place with Pilot Officer Ferić, Flying Officer Januszewicz and Pilot Officer Walters walking on left.

POLISH SQUADRONS ENTERING THE BATTLE

Opposite above: The last salute to the fallen. In time the PAF Section of Northwood Cemetery would expand…

Opposite below: Unidentified Hurricane I with Warrant Officer Kazimierz Mozół standing in front of it and Corporal Franciszek Gurzyński sitting on its port wing. Note that one of the engine cover panels has been replaced.

Below: A group photo of 303 Squadron flying and ground personnel taken between 27 September as Paszkiewicz is missing from this picture and 8 October when František, who is proudly wearing Virtuti Militari Cross, seated in the middle in front of Kellett and Urbanowicz, was killed. Another example of how freely dress code was treated even at this late stage of the Battle of Britain. Sitting in second row from left, Zumbach (5th), Wodecki (6th), Pisarek (7th), Henneberg (13th) as well as Bełc (8th from right in 3rd row) are wearing their 'beloved' French flying jackets. At the same time Wiórkiewicz (4th), who was a Technical Officer, is wearing a Polish pilot's badge! Mierzwa (16th) still has his French service cap with Polish podporucznik rank's star while Grzeszczak (17th) wears a dark shirt! Ferić (1st from right) is back in Polish-style uniform and Karubin and Szaposznikow (standing in 3rd row as 7th and 10th from right) are stubbornly wearing their Polish and RAF wings. Furthermore, there are some of 303 Squadron's men wearing berets, others have service caps without badges, some others are presenting 1919 RAF uniforms. Pilot Officer Palusiński (sitting 2nd from right in 2nd row), although he flew eleven operational sorties during the Battle of Britain, is very rarely mentioned in publications. He was one of the Polish pilots who joined 303 Squadron right after their arrival from France and were posted to 5 OTU for Hurricane conversion, therefore he missed a big part of the Battle. In Poland Palusiński claimed the first victory for 111th Squadron (303's predecessor) on 1 September 1939, but was also its first pilot to be shot down. Despite being badly injured he was able to leave Poland. His wounds, however, did not heal completely and after leaving 303 Squadron, he never flew operationally again, serving in various Ops Rooms.

Above: Flying Officer Wacław Łapkowski was shot down in Hurricane I P2985 RF-Z on 5 September 1940. Badly burnt and with a broken left hand, he spent a few months recovering, before being able to rejoin 303 Squadron in January 1941. Here he is photographed at the RAF Convalescent Centre in Torquay with Jerzy Bajan, who was commanding officer of the Air Force Cadet Officers' School in Dęblin when the war broke out. He was badly wounded by bomb shrapnel in left hand on 2 September 1939, hence he is wearing a glove in this picture. This disability should have eliminated him from flying, yet in Britain he used a hook attached to his arm that helped him to fly again, including a few operational sorties. Bajan later became Polish Liaison Officer with Fighter Command, replacing Pawlikowski who was killed in action.

Opposite above: Here, both officers are joined by another victim of the Battle of Britain. Pilot Officer Stanisław Łapka from 302 Squadron, who is sitting far left, broke his right leg after bailing out from his Hurricane V6569 WX-K on 15 September 1940. 'Mały' ('Little'), as Łapka was known, due to his short posture, arrived at Newquay on 8 October. Note Łapkowski's Silver Cross of Virtuti Militari which he was awarded with while being away from Northolt and presumably delivered by Bajan in October 1940, when this picture was taken.

Opposite below: Łapkowski, who is standing in the middle, accompanied by his local sweetheart and two RAF officers. Pilot Officer Robert McGovan, far left, of 92 Squadron was shot down on 14 September 1940 and on 11 October he was admitted to Newquay Convalescent Centre. Australian Pilot Officer Harry Hardman's (right) presence here is not clear. He left No. 111 Squadron on 8 September 1940 and rejoined this unit on 3 January 1941. No information on his injuries can be found so far.

Another interesting picture of Łapkowski (1st left) taken while in Newquay. Here, he is accompanied by Pilot Officer Alexander Zatonski (aka Aleksander Zatoński) of 79 Squadron (2nd left). Zatonski was born in Philadelphia, USA, in a family of Polish immigrants, and during his youth visited Poland several times. It is said that until high school he spoke very little English, and tried to join the Polish Air Force to fight the Germans. Eventually he was accepted by the RAF, and was shot down on 28 August 1940. Note the white glove he is wearing as he was badly burned, and also wounded in the leg. When he sent this photo to his parents, he assured them in Polish that he was wearing a glove, not a bandage; he also described the building in the background as a hotel, probably not to scare his mother.

One more photo of Polish fighter pilots taken in Newquay during the Battle of Britain.

After midday on 6 October 1940 a single Ju 88 from 4./KG30 strafed Northolt airfield, machine gunning buildings and hangars, killing a member of the British ground crew. The German crew also dropped two bombs and as result two Polish Hurricanes were hit. Flying Officer Wiórkiewicz, an Engineering Officer, and two of his men showed extreme bravery by trying to save these aircraft. Corporal Władysław Roubo risked his life by switching off the engine of P3217 RF-S when the bomb exploded 10 metres from him. Warrant Officer Józef Mikołajczak was sitting on the wing of P3120 RF-A as only minutes before he had been helping its pilot to synchronise the machine guns.

Above: How Mikołajczak survived the blast when an aircraft was directly hit remains a mystery. According to some sources, RF-A's pilot Sergeant Antoni Siudak was taxiing his machine and moving it away from the area of attack, hence he died when the bomb exploded. Others claim that he was blown by the blast onto the tarmac, fracturing his skull. Siudak previously flew with 302 Squadron and on 15 September he shared the destruction of a Do 17. On 21 September he joined 303 Squadron and added two Bf 109s and one shared Bf 110 only one day before his death. The state of the wreckage does not allow us to assess whether it had either the checkerboard or/and an inscription mentioned by Urbanowicz.

Opposite below: The day after the tragedy Arkady Fiedler, well known Polish writer and adventurer, visited Northolt for the first time. He was there to watch and listen to Polish pilots and mechanics as he was looking for inspiration for his book 'Squadron 303'. His work was published soon after, making 'Kościuszko' Squadron even more famous and immortal. The names of the main characters, though, were changed to protect the safety of pilots' relatives living back in occupied Poland.

232

Sergeant Antoni Siudak.

Above: The most iconic, yet staged, photo of 303 Squadron pilots pretending to be 'returning' from an operation was taken after unit's move to RAF Leconfield. Unsurprisingly, Urbanowicz is missing from the group as he had already left command, taking the role of Polish Liaison Officer of 11 Group. After close inspection we can see a variety of uniforms being worn, even at this last stage of the Battle of Britain. From left are: Pilot Officer Ferić, wearing a French-made Polish uniform with RAF buttons (!), Flight Lieutenant Kent, Flying Officer Grzeszczak and Pilot Officer Jerzy Radomski, who previously fought over Poland and France. Radomski arrived at Northolt on 21 August but soon after was posted to 5 OTU. He rejoined 303 on 27 September and three days later he shared a victory over a Do 17, and made a forced landing in P3663 RF-H. Then there is Pilot Officer Zumbach (surprise, surprise!) marching in a French jacket, Pilot Officer Mierzwa (obscured by Pilot Officer Łokuciewski, Flying Officer Henneberg, Sergeants Rogowski and Szaposznikow. Rogowski arrived from 74 Squadron, where he had also flown in combat. The latter was the only Polish pilot who flew operationally two different types of fighters during the Battle of Britain, swapping Spitfires for Hurricanes. The Hurricane in the background is V6684 RF-F, but the famous '126 Adolfs' and 'The Polish Squadron' slogans, both chalked near the squadron emblem, are not added yet. Instead an attempt to write something else on the engine's cowling had been made.

Here the same mysterious motif is unfortunately obscured by the group of armourers.

The same aircraft poses with a smaller group of pilots: Ferić, Grzeszczak, Zumbach, Henneberg and the adopted 'Pole' Kent(owski). Three of them made their kills flying this Hurricane. V6684 arrived in mid-September and despite being damaged twice it remained with 303 until 27 October, gaining spectacular results: A/Squadron Leader Urbanowicz destroyed two Do 17s on 15 September, Pilot Officer Zumbach shot down one Bf 109 and one He 111 on 26 September, then added one Bf 109 a day after; Flight Lieutenant Kent downed one Ju 88 on 27 September and finally Flying Officer Henneberg reported one Bf 110 on 5 October.

Another photo of 303 pilots, where Zumbach's affection for French fashion can be visible. Many years after the war he ran a night club in Paris, among many other adventures.

POLISH SQUADRONS ENTERING THE BATTLE

Opposite above: Three Battle of Poland, France and Britain veterans posing with V6684. Sergeants Szaposznikow, Karubin and Wünsche, with the latter wearing long Polish flying jacket.

Opposite below: Flying Officer Marian Pisarek (1st right) inherited B Flight, which he commanded following Paszkiewicz's death, but also Witold Urbanowicz's Mae West with the latter's 'W.U.' initials. Pisarek, the former 141st Fighter Squadron commander that operated from Toruń, hence, generally speaking, one of the 'outsiders' in 303 Squadron, was shot down on 7 September. He bailed out leaving a shoe inside Hurricane I R4173 RF-T, which crashed at 40 Roding Road, Laughton, killing three civilians. Pisarek's shoe, together with pieces of his aircraft, was recovered in 1976. He was lost in action on 29 April 1942 commanding 1 Polish Wing. Flight Lieutenant Kent, who is standing in the middle, left 303 on 24 October to take command of 92 Squadron.

Below: One more famous photo taken at Leconfield with Zumbach, Ferić and squadron mascot, a little Alsatian puppy. Mirosław Ferić is wearing the black Omega 6B/159 watch that some of the RAF members were issued with. He was promoted to Flying Officer rank on 27 October, a few days after this picture was taken, but as he liked wearing this foreign tunic, it would not be adorned with RAF ranks. Ferić brought this uniform from France, where he swapped the original Polish buttons with one of the RAF airmen and sewed them on to make a strange combination. Although selling Polish and French leather jackets, as well as buttons, proved to be a lucrative business for some time, especially for the airmen who, during those early days, were short of money, Zumbach seems to like his French jacket. Close inspection reveals that '126 Adolfs', and 'The Polish Squadron', had been applied onto the fuselage.

Above: Polish and British ground crews with Hurricane V6684 RF-F adorned with the squadron's 126 kills chalked on its fuselage.

Opposite above: Close up where Hitler's caricature is also visible: '126 Adolfs', which symbolised 303's Battle of Britain total score. The first photographic evidence, known so far, of a Polish-flown Hurricane adorned with aerial victories.[8]

Opposite below left: Three lesser known pilots of 303 Squadron. Sergeant Henryk Skowron flew one operational sortie during the Battle of Britain.

Opposite below right: Sergeant Leon Świtoń was initially posted to 54 Squadron RAF where he flew two missions on 15 August 1940, before joining 'Kościuszko' Squadron.

---

8. Less than a year later Flying Officer Henryk Szczęsny, a Battle of Britain veteran, decorated his personal Hurricane JH-S (presumably Z3975) of No. 317 (Polish) Squadron with two swastikas. These were his kills claimed while in 'City of Wilno' Squadron and his previous victories, including these from Poland and Battle of Britain, were not applied.

POLES IN THE BATTLE OF BRITAIN

Above: Pilot Officer Andrzej Malarowski's log book is the only document that confirms his one operational sortie during the Battle of Britain.

Opposite above: Resting at Leconfield was a good opportunity for newly arrived pilots, with combat experience from Poland, France or from both, to gain more familiarity flying British equipment. Luckily for Pilot Officer Tadeusz Sawicz (5th from left) it was also a chance to fly an operational sortie, which qualified him for Battle of Britain participant status. In general, 303 Squadron became slightly overcrowded with more pilots arriving. From left are: Pilot Officer Jerzy Radomski, Flying Officer Władysław Szczęśniewski, Pilot Officer Jan Zumbach, Flying Officer Bohdan Grzeszczak, Pilot Officers Tadeusz Sawicz, Witold Łokuciewski, Bogusław Mierzwa, Flying Officer Zdzisław Henneberg, Flight Lieutenant John Kent, Sergeant Eugeniusz Szaposznikow, Flying Officer Marian Pisarek (behind Szaposznikow), Sergeants Mirosław Wojciechowski, Marian Rytka (behind Wojciechowski), Sergeants Franciszek Prętkiewicz, Stanisław Karubin, Marian Bełc, Bronisław Kościk, Stanisław Brzeski, Wacław Giermer, Kazimierz Wünsche, Jozef Káňa (Slovak pilot who also flew with 303 Squadron during Battle of Britain) and Jan Rogowski.

Flying Officer Jan Bury-Burzyński, another Polish Campaign 1939 veteran with two kills, did not fly operationally during the Battle of Britain, undergoing training in 303 Squadron from 12 October 1940. He was killed twelve days later in a flying accident when his Hurricane I R6807 RF-R crashed at Bishop Burton, Beverley. Consequently, Bury-Burzyński was the last 303's flying loss during the Battle of Britain.

303 Squadron Hurricanes with quick recognition markings that were introduced in November 1940. However, aircraft P3383 RF-T pictured here was flown from the end of September 1940, after replacing L1696 in which Flying Officer Paszkiewicz was killed. On 1 October, Flying Officer Januszewicz flew its first patrol and from then it was used operationally by Flight Lieutenants Forbes, Pisarek, Pilot Officer Mierzwa, Flight Sergeant Káňa, Sergeants Kowalski, Palak and Wojciechowski.

Sergeant Jan Palak flew in both Polish fighter squadrons during the Battle of Britain.

Above and below: Hurricane I V7624 RF-B was delivered to Leconfield very close to the end of Battle of Britain and was taken for a non-operational flight for the first time by Sergeant Prętkiewicz on 25 October.

Three ground crew members including one pretending to be a pilot with unknown Hurricane, most probably RF-H or RF-U.

Poor quality photo that shows three Hurricanes including N2460 RF-D and N2661 RF-J, all with Sky spinner and tail band, as well as black under surfaces of port wings. All these changes were introduced after the Battle of Britain, yet these two aircraft flew in 303 Squadron during the Battle. N2460 arrived at Northolt on 30 September and on the same day it was flown by Squadron Leader Kellett twice. On 5 October this aircraft was flown by Sergeant Siudak when he claimed the shared destruction of a Bf 110 and then two Bf 109s. The latter flew this mount a few times before that day. N2661 also was delivered to 'Kościuszko' Squadron on 30 September and did not achieve any combat success, apart from one Bf 109 erroneously added by the clerk to Pilot Officer Palusiński's name on 7 October. It was used operationally for the first time on 1 October – twice by Pilot Officer Ferić. N2661 was also flown during patrols by A/Squadron Leader Urbanowicz, Flight Lieutenant Kent, Flying Officer Grzeszczak, Pilot Officers Palusiński, Radomski and Sergeant Szaposznikow. Third in line is Hurricane I V7244 RF-C, a true workhorse and veteran that flew in 303 Squadron from the early days until the end of the Battle of Britain. This aircraft was never damaged in combat, yet brought down six Bf 109s, two Bf 110s and one Do 17.

After 303 Squadron had been transferred further north, apart from usual fighter patrols, its pilots were involved in training of newcomers. The new arrivals weren't greenhorns at all, most of them fought over Poland or France, some of them even flew during the Battle of Britain in RAF squadrons. They only needed some final touches before being posted to other units. From the left standing are: Sergeant Edward Paterek who initially fought in 302 Squadron before being posted to 303 Squadron and flew over thirty sorties during the Battle of Britain, scoring twice; Flying Officer Zbigniew Kustrzyński, another Battle of Britain pilot of 111 and 607 Squadrons,[9] Sergeant Marian Bełc, Flying Officer Wiktor Strzembosz, Flying Officer Eugeniusz Fiedorczuk, Flying Officer Wojciech Kołaczkowski, Flying Officer Włodzimierz Miksa, who after an initial stay in 151 Squadron joined 303 Squadron, flew once during the Battle of Britain and was wounded while landing; Squadron Leader Adam Kowalczyk, new 303 commander, Pilot Officer Jerzy Radomski, Flight Lieutenant Witold Żyborski, Group Captain Stefan Pawlikowski, former commander of Pursuit Brigade, now Polish Senior Liaison Officer at HQ of Fighter Command; Flying Officer Wieńczysław Barański who managed to fly once during the Battle of Britain while in 607 Squadron, Flying Officer Bohdan Grzeszczak, Flight Lieutenant Francis Brinsden, new A Flight commander, Pilot Officer Józef Czachowski, Flight Lieutenant Ian Hallam (?), Flying Officer Jerzy Jankiewicz who arrived from 601 Squadron where he fought bravely during the Battle of Britain, Pilot Officer Franciszek Kornicki, Squadron Leader Witold Urbanowicz, former 303 Squadron commander, now serving in 11 Group, Flying Officer Tadeusz Arentowicz, Flying Officer Zdzisław Henneberg, Flying Officer Jan Zumbach, Flying Officer Aleksander Gabszewicz with two operational sorties in 607 Squadron during the Battle of Britain, and Flying Officer Mirosław Feriç. Crouching in first line are: Sergeants Stanisław Wieraszka, Eugeniusz Szaposznikow, Stanisław Karubin, Kazimierz Wünsche, Jozef Káňa and Jan Kowalski.

---

9. Initially, in July 1940, he was considered for 303 Squadron.

Twenty-nine years after the Battle of Britain another picture was taken of what was supposed to be a 303 Squadron Hurricane. On this occasion it was one of the aircraft used during the making of the film 'Battle of Britain'. Although the historical accuracy of its scheme and marking was far from correct, H3421 MI-D played its part rather well as a reminder of the brave Poles who fought in the skies over Britain in 1940.

Index

INDEX